"Honor is a *decision* we make to place high value, worth, and importance on another person by viewing him or her as a priceless gift and granting that person a position in our lives worthy of great respect . . ."

—Gary Smalley and John Trent

GARY SMALLEY, president of Today's Family in Phoenix, holds a bachelor's degree in psychology and has a master of divinity degree from Bethel Seminary in St. Paul, Minnesota. His previous bestselling books include *If Only He Knew, For Better or Best* and *The Key to Your Child's Heart*. He and John Trent team-teach the *Love Is a Decision* seminar in cities across the United States and Canada. Gary and his wife, Norma, are the parents of three children, Kari, Greg and Michael.

JOHN TRENT, vice president of Today's Family, works in partnership with Gary Smalley. He has a Ph.D. in marriage and family counseling and holds a master's degree in New Testament Greek from Dallas Theological Seminary. He co-authored with Gary the bestselling books *The Blessing, The Gift of Honor, The Language of Love* and *Love Is a Decision*. He lives in Phoenix with his wife, Cynthia, and daughter, Kari Lorraine.

Books by Gary Smalley and John Trent

The Blessing
The Gift of Honor

Published by POCKET BOOKS

Most Pocket Books are available at special quantity discounts for bulk purchases for sales promotions, premiums or fund raising. Special books or book excerpts can also be created to fit specific needs.

For details write the office of the Vice President of Special Markets, Pocket Books, 1230 Avenue of the Americas, New York, New York 10020.

The Gift of Honor

Gary Smalley & John Trent, Ph.D.

POCKET BOOKS

New York London Toronto Sydney Tokyo Singapore

Scripture quotations are from THE NEW KING JAMES VERSION
of the Bible. Copyright © 1979, 1980, 1982, Thomas Nelson, Inc.,
Publishers.

POCKET BOOKS, a division of Simon & Schuster Inc.
1230 Avenue of the Americas, New York, NY 10020

Copyright © 1987 by Gary Smalley and John Trent

All rights reserved, including the right to reproduce
this book or portions thereof in any form whatsoever.
For information address Thomas Nelson, Inc.,
Nelson Place at Elm Hill Pike, Nashville, TN 37214

ISBN: 0-671-69032-9

First Pocket Books printing November 1990

10 9 8 7 6 5 4 3 2

POCKET and colophon are registered trademarks of
Simon & Schuster Inc.

Printed in the U.S.A.

This book is dedicated to Zoa Trent, John's mother. A tremendous model of a parent who honors her children, she was a great help on this book.

Acknowledgments

We would like to express our deepest thanks to the following people:

To Darryl DelHousaye, Bill Yarger, and Tom Rietveld, three of our supportive pastors in our home church who took the time to review and critique this book and offer their suggestions.

To Doug Childress for again being a loving "critic" and a great source of encouragement.

To Diana Trent, for her hard work in proofreading the manuscript.

To Larry Weeden, Susan Salmon, and the rest of the editorial staff at Thomas Nelson for working so diligently with us in meeting deadlines.

To Terry Brown, our teammate in ministry, for covering even more bases than usual while we were away writing this book.

To Ken Gire at Insight for Living and Steve Laube at our local Christian bookstore for taking time out of very busy schedules to give us their wisdom and insights into the concept of honor.

And to Wendy Ragan, our dear friend at Thomas Nelson, who has been such an encouragement to us and to many other authors at Thomas Nelson over the years.

Contents

CONTENTS

Preface

Whether we realize it or not, the value we attach to God, our children, and ourselves can greatly determine the success or failure of all our relationships. Indeed, nothing will do more to build healthy families than learning to give and receive the gift of honor.

No matter how old our children are, it's never too late to start honoring them. As we learn more about the biblical concept of honor and as we apply this principle, we do all we can to save our children the heartbreak of damaged relationships. We give them the foundation they will need to develop a deeper maturity when leaving home and cleaving to their mates.

If you would like more information about the authors' national speaking schedule or other books and cassette tapes, please write to:

Today's Family, P.O. Box 22111, Phoenix, AZ 85028.

The Gift of Honor

CHAPTER ONE

Joining the Battle

Something took place in the fall of 1944 that can explain a major reason many children are facing a losing battle in today's families. It was late October when an officer commanding a platoon of American soldiers received a call from headquarters. Over the radio, this captain learned his unit was being ordered to recapture a small French city from the Nazis—and he learned something else from headquarters as well. For weeks, French Resistance fighters had risked their lives to gather information about the German fortifications in that city, and they had smuggled this information out to the Allies.

The French Underground's efforts had provided the Americans with something worth its weight in gold: a detailed map of the city. It wasn't just a map with the names of major streets and landmarks; it showed specific details of the enemy's defensive positions.

Indeed, the map even identified shops and buildings where German soldiers bunked or where a machine-gun nest or a sniper had been stationed. Block by block, the Frenchmen gave an accounting of the German units and the gun emplacements they manned.

For a captain who was already concerned about mounting casualty lists, receiving such information was an answer to prayer. Although the outcome of the war wouldn't depend on this one skirmish, to him it meant that he wouldn't

1

have to write as many letters to his men's parents or wives telling them their loved one had been cut down in battle.

Before the soldiers moved out to take their objective, the captain gave each man a chance to study the map. And wanting to make sure his men read it carefully, he hurriedly gave them a test covering the major landmarks and enemy strongholds. Just before his platoon moved out, the officer graded the tests, and with minor exceptions every man earned a perfect score. As a direct result of having that map to follow, the men captured the city with little loss of American lives.

Nearly thirty years after this military operation took place, an army researcher heard the story and decided to base a study on it.[1] The project began in France, where instead of a platoon of soldiers, he arranged for a group of American tourists to help him with his research.

For several hours, the men and women were allowed to study the same map the soldiers had, and then they were given the same test. You can guess the results. Most of the tourists failed miserably.

The reason for the difference between these two groups was obvious—motivation. Knowing their lives were on the line, the soldiers were highly motivated to learn every detail of the map. For the tourists, being in a research study provided some motivation. But most of them had nothing to lose but a little pride if they failed the test.

What does this story have to do with honoring our children? Actually, a great deal. What took place in that village years ago is applicable to the war taking place in many homes and affecting many children today.

In our secular society, when it comes to the battle our children face with feeling insignificant and of low value, many of us act like tourists. With all the intensity of people on a month-long vacation, many of us look at the Scriptures or a Christian book as we do passing scenery through a car window. Not realizing what's at stake, we expend little energy on discovering and putting into practice specific ways to value our children. Little do we know that many sons and daughters, perhaps a child living right under our own roof, may be under tremendous attack in a losing battle to honor God, themselves, or others.

Thankfully, not all parents are so naive. Just the fact that you're reading a book like this marks you as concerned and special! Like the soldiers who knew what was at stake in studying that map, some parents have the motivation and desire to learn how to raise their children's sense of value.

What we hope to do in this book is to alert parents to the battle going on in many children's lives and to the terrible results that can come from experiencing the emotional wounds of a dishonoring home. Even more, our desire is to provide parents with a detailed map that points out not only enemy strongholds to avoid but also seven different safety zones that moms and dads can use to build high value in their children.

In calling parents to arms, we're certainly not saying that this is the "final" book on building self-worth in a child or loved one. Of first importance we have the Scriptures, and there are many other good, biblically based books that can help us encourage our children.[2] Yet regardless of what books we take down from the shelf, we need to have an intensity and a willingness to learn and apply biblical principles. Only then can we attack a problem that can emotionally cripple our children.

BLESSING CHILDREN AND BEYOND

How serious a problem is growing up without love and acceptance? Is it really a "battle" our children face or simply an insignificant skirmish?

Several months ago, we looked at these very questions in a book we wrote called *The Blessing*. In that book, we looked at the Old Testament concept of "blessing" children and what it was like for children today to grow up with or without their parents' love and acceptance. In particular, we discussed five specific things parents did in biblical times, and could do today, to attach high value to their children. We also looked at several homes that commonly

3

withhold this blessing and the emotional damage that often faces children who grow up in them.

Since that book was published, we have been flooded with letters and calls from men and women who have told us their tragic stories, and even more tragic results, of missing out on their families' blessing. And while we knew from our counseling and conferences that this was a problem, we had no idea how deeply it ran and how many people it affected.

While *The Blessing* seemed to unearth this problem and gave parents several practical ways they could encourage and build up their children, we began looking in the Scriptures for additional tools they could use. Our search led us to study in depth the concept of "honor" and, as a result, to seven additional steps parents can take to build a lasting sense of love and acceptance into their children. Unfortunately, it also taught us more than we wanted to know about the devastating results of growing up in a "dishonoring" home.

How deeply can it hurt a child to grow up being dishonored and feeling of little worth to parents and other loved ones? Just ask Denny. Years of living in just such an environment not only significantly damaged him in all his relationships, but also brought him to the breaking point one winter night.

THE DAMAGING RESULTS OF
A DISHONORING HOME

Football practice was over, and Denny was sore from head to toe. He walked slowly down the rows of aging apartment buildings, each drab gray in the fading winter sun. Coming to his own building, he pushed open the heavy aluminum door and began to walk slowly up the two flights of stairs to his family's apartment. The stairway walls were covered with years of graffiti and holes where the plaster had been torn loose, yet nothing caught Denny's attention—until he reached the second floor landing.

Suddenly, his head shot up and his schoolbooks dropped from his hands. Shivers ran up and down his body as he heard through the apartment door the all too familiar sounds of his mother's screaming.

For years Denny had tried to calm his father during his many angry rampages. His dad's drunken fits of rage usually left one of Denny's brothers or sisters (or more often his mother) black and blue. Yet this time would be different. This was the last straw!

An award-winning football player in a city famous for hard-nosed athletes, Denny ripped open the door and charged at his dad. Not caring about the consequences of his actions, he could only think of the times he had been brutalized by his father.

As a boy growing up, Denny could never find a place safe from his father's anger. He had tried hiding under the house, and his father found and beat him. Another time, he had crawled into the narrow space between the refrigerator and the kitchen cabinet to hide, but his father discovered him and kicked him into the corner until he finally tired of the sport. Too many nights, his mother would meet him at the door, and the family would drive around town, waiting for his father to get so drunk he finally passed out.

This had to stop. Although Denny was several inches shorter than his father, working with weights had made him stronger than his dad, who had been a steel worker for years. Now, his eyes red with fury and his adrenaline pumping, Denny tore his father off his mother. He hit him twice in quick succession, and as his father reeled back, he screamed and rammed into his father like a raging bull, knocking him to the floor. Then, with years of burning memories giving him lion-like strength, he lifted his father and threw him through the second-story window.

The deafening sounds of shattering glass, his mother's screaming, and his father's crashing from an aluminum canopy down to the yard below echoed inside the room. Denny ran down the stairs and over to his father, who was already sitting up in the yard. They were amazed to see that although his father was shaken and had a number of superficial cuts, nothing was broken. Grabbing his father by the front of his shirt, Denny pulled him up and with cold fury spat the words into his face, "If you ever touch any of us again, I'll kill you!"

Shortly after this incident, Denny left home for good, but no matter how far he traveled, he never escaped its memories. Because he had come from a dishonoring home, he knew how to live with anger and mistrust, but not with warmth and love. Every relationship Denny entered—including two marriages and a string of friendships shattered by his fiery temper—turned into a repeat performance of the tragedy he had left behind. Unfortunately, at the root of many of his problems was alcoholism—something Denny had sworn would never destroy his life as it had his father's.

Just another story of someone with a tragic background? Hardly. In the last chapter of this book, we'll reveal what Denny learned during the lowest point in his life that totally turned him around. What he learned and decided to apply in his life is what this book is all about.

Through a caring friend at work, Denny learned for the first time what it meant to give honor to God and how, for most of his life, he had done nothing but dishonor Him. All his life he had longed to be valued and accepted, and now he discovered the very source of significance and life itself.

Not only did Denny learn to honor God, but he also learned to apply honor to each of his important relationships. Denny discovered that instead of being an abstract concept, honor was something he could and should give to his wife, his children, his friends—and miraculously—even to his father. As Denny learned about the positive benefits of honoring God and others, his life changed so dramatically that years after throwing his father through a window, he was able to call him on the phone and tell him he loved him—an event that opened the door to dramatic changes in his dad's life.

A NEEDED INGREDIENT IN EVERYDAY HOMES

We realize that Denny's story represents an extreme. Thankfully, most parents do their best to genuinely love their children, and most children never have to face the degree of dishonor and hurt that Denny did. However, all parents need to know what actions honor their children and which ones lower their sense of self-worth.

You might be thinking, *But my little Jimmy and Suzy are doing great! Why do I need to invest time in learning to combat a problem they're not even facing today?*

What we have discovered in talking with people across the country is that the results of dishonoring parental actions accumulate over time. On numerous occasions, we have counseled with well-meaning mothers and fathers who sat in our office in bewilderment and shock over their son or daughter's self-destructive behavior. Others have been just as shocked when they discovered drug abuse, promiscuity, or other damaging patterns in their children's lives.

As youngsters, many of these children showed little or no evidence of the problems they face as adolescents today. And very often as we began to look back into the history of these children, we found that their parents had no idea of honoring actions they were leaving out of their children's lives and dishonoring actions they were allowing to accumulate.

During World War II, Winston Churchill said, "All that has to happen for evil to prevail in the world is for good men to do nothing." In our twisted society today, parents need more than simply good intentions when it comes to raising secure, confident children—they need a plan. And while things may be going well today, we need to take the offensive to understand what it means to honor our children and raise their sense of self-worth and what actions to avoid that can lower it.

"It could never happen to my child!" some might say. Let's look, however, at some of the problems children from "average" homes often face, children whose parents never understood the tragic results of their dishonoring actions.

COMMON EFFECTS OF DISHONORING HOMES

- Drug and alcohol abuse[3]
- Chronic lying[4]
- Procrastination[5]
- Extreme pride and self-centeredness (narcissism)[6]
- Workaholism and the need to achieve more and more[7]
- Vicious emotional cycles[8]
- Repeated absences from church and school[9]
- Extreme submission[10]
- Unhealthy legalism[11]
- Severe withdrawal from society[12]
- Sexual difficulties in marriage[13]
- Lower academic achievement[14]
- Feelings of loss of control[15]
- Stress-related heart problems[16]
- Homosexuality[17]
- Deep feelings of loneliness[18]
- Suicidal thinking and attempts[19]
- Problems with delinquency[20]
- Poor mate selection in marriage[21]
- Clinical depression[22]
- Poor decision making[23]
- Lowered career achievement[24]
- A pattern of outbursts of anger[25]
- Low energy in accomplishing school or work tasks[26]
- Extreme self-criticism[27]
- Gravitation toward cults and fringe religious groups[28]
- Having unrealistic expectations of self and others[29]

Emotionally healthy parents wouldn't want to see their children experience the terrible heartache represented in these problems. Yet without realizing it, some parents lead their children down these very paths.

How can we work to avoid these things in our children's lives? How can we do battle against such problems and build value into their lives? At the heart of making our children or anyone else feel valuable, loved, and accepted is a decision to *honor* them.

THE GIFT OF HONOR

When you think of what it means to honor someone, what may come to mind is attending a retirement party, meeting the president, or standing with a crowd of fans cheering for a favorite team after they've won "the" game. It's also normal to think of it as something that goes only in one direction—usually toward a superior or someone who has "earned" or "deserves" it. However, as you will see throughout this book, when the Scriptures talk about giving honor to God or to loved ones, they don't leave such a fuzzy definition. Instead, they give a crystal clear picture that honoring someone involves viewing him as a priceless treasure and treating him with loving respect. They also show that while honoring God is based on His worthiness, honoring others is something that can be passed on to loved ones regardless of whether they "deserve" it or not. We believe the next statement summarizes this entire book:

> **Honor is a decision we make to place high value, worth, and importance on another person by viewing him or her as a priceless gift and granting him or her a position in our lives worthy of great respect; and Love involves putting that decision into action.**

When Jesus was asked to name the great commandments in the Scriptures, He didn't hesitate in the least. He told a young lawyer, "Love the LORD your God with all your heart, with all your soul, and with all your mind. . . . You shall love your neighbor as yourself."[30] Loving God, loving others, and finding value in ourselves. Without a doubt, these three aspects of love are the most effective weapons against the destructive power of low self-worth, and communicating loving actions is what this book is all about.

Genuine love is a gift we give others. It isn't purchased by their actions or contingent upon our emotions at the moment. It may carry with it strong emotional feelings, but it isn't supported by them. Rather, it is a decision we make on a daily basis that someone is special and valuable to us.

Like genuine love, honor is a gift we give to someone. It involves the decision we make *before* we put love into action that a person is of high value. In fact, love for someone often begins to flow once we have made the decision to honor him.

Our goal in this book is to combat low self-worth by explaining how to treasure our loved ones and how to communicate to them that they have a special place in our lives. As we've seen in Denny's case and in each of the effects of a dishonoring home, this is especially important for children. When we give our children the gift of honor—that is, when we learn how to communicate to them in tangible ways that they are deeply loved and highly valued—it goes a long way toward combating future problems in their lives.

That's why we're excited about sharing with you a practical definition of what it means to honor others and seven ways you can apply it in their lives. These are seven aspects of honor that you can apply and act out on a daily basis and raise your children's value as a result. These are honoring attitudes that can shape parenting actions and encourage children. These *aren't* a seven-part formula or seven simple, foolproof steps. Each of the seven aspects of honor will be expanded in a later section of the book.

We give our children the gift of honor by . . .
- extending it first to our own parents.
- helping them find value in troubled times.
- recognizing our own parenting strengths and style.
- providing a healthy balance in our homes.
- establishing loving boundaries.
- building positive loyalties.
- offering honor to God.

While we'll be directing these seven aspects of honor primarily toward our children, they can help us enrich each of our relationships. They can help us increase our value of God and enable us to learn what it means to honor a spouse. Friends can give honor to one another, and churches to those they seek to minister to. Employees can find a new reason to value their employers, and employers to respect their employees.

GETTING BACK TO THE BATTLE

We began this chapter by sounding the call for parents to join the battle against a major destroyer of children—their feeling valueless and insignificant. We can't stress enough how important each day is in waging this war. If we sit back, fold our hands, and neglect building self-worth in our children, one day King Solomon's words may come true in their lives or our own. When this wise king wrote about the sluggard, he made this comment:

> *A little sleep, a little slumber,*
> *A little folding of the hands to rest;*
> *So your poverty will come like a prowler,*
> *And your want like an armed man.*[31]

If we act like tourists or sluggards when it comes to building value into our children, heartache may enter our homes as stealthily as a prowler, or discouragement may burst upon us as forcefully as an armed man.

No matter how old your children are, it's never too late to unfold your hands and start honoring them. When you consistently apply this concept, you save them the heartache of damaged relationships, and you also give them the foundation they will need to truly value God, themselves, and others.

Parents, do your children (and yourself) a great favor. Give them a gift that can strengthen them their entire lives—a gift that can continue to build up and bless your children and even your grandchildren—*the gift of honor*.

Where do we begin? By getting a clear picture of a key marked "honor," and understanding how dishonoring our own parents can lock the door to building value into our children.

CHAPTER TWO

The Gift of Honor

Have you ever been handed the wrong key to a hotel room? Regardless of how much effort you may put into opening the door to your room, or how sincere you are about its working, if the desk clerk hands you a poorly cut key or one that fits a different door, you're sincerely wrong when you try to use it.

The same thing is true of building value into your children. It's not enough that you are handed a set of keys or principles to unlock the door to self-worth. If they aren't cut correctly or are missing a few of the teeth that match the lock, they may open another door, but they won't fit the one marked "self-worth."

That's why we want to take a close look at the biblical concept of honor as we begin this book. If a key isn't cut accurately, it doesn't matter how practical it is. We want to make sure that you're making proper use of the key marked "honor" and that you can spot a counterfeit key named "dishonor."

We know that definitions can bore some people, but we feel strongly that getting a clear idea of what it means to honor God or loved ones is at the heart of all healthy relationships. With that in mind, let's look more closely at the concept itself and at how it can be applied in the home.

We'll look first at the opposite of honor, namely, dishonor. By contrasting the two, we can gain insight into what honor avoids, as well as what it builds, in a person's life.

AS LITTLE VALUE AS A VAPOR

A few months ago, we flew over to southern California to be on our good friend, Al Sander's, radio program, "Vox-Pop." After we had finished the program (and our favorite chicken dinner at Knott's Berry Farm), we hustled to the airport to catch our plane.

When we arrived, we discovered that all air traffic was being delayed by a light mist that had drifted in from the ocean. As we sat in the terminal and waited to board our plane, we watched that light mist turn into a gripping fog, closing down the airport and forcing us to spend another night in California.

Who would have thought that something as insignificant as a little mist could have turned into a major problem that disrupted our schedules, inconvenienced hundreds of other people, and proved costly to the airlines? Just a vapor! Yet it had the power to disrupt so many schedules and lives.

We see a similar occurrence in family relationships. People who grow up feeling worthless and unlovable—those who were dishonored in their home—have usually grown up in an environment where unloving acts have surrounded them like a vapor.

Like the mist that drifts in from the ocean at night, dishonoring actions by a parent may start with a critical word or an angry glance—not cause for major problems at first. But if left unchecked, one day that mist can build up and turn into a gripping fog. That disabling fog of hurtful words and actions can become self-destructive to children, creating boys and girls who grow up with damaged emotions and problems in future intimate relationships.

In the Scriptures, the word *dishonor* is used of "something or someone who has little worth, weight, or value."[1] One word picture used to describe it is the same one we faced at the airport and some children face at home—a "mist or vapor."[2] In one instance, it was used to describe the steam that rises from a boiling pot of water.[3]

When the Greeks thought of a word picture to describe something of the least value imaginable, they thought of mist or steam. It referred to something of such little weight and significance that it was good only to be waved or wiped away as a nuisance.

In relationships, when we dishonor people, we consciously or unconsciously treat them as if they have as little weight or value as a vapor. When do we treat someone like that? How about when a preschooler has just asked the same question for the thousandth time; a youngster leaves his toys out at night again so that others trip over them in the dark; a teen-ager seems to selectively forget what he's been told; a spouse has the nerve to try and ask a question or to do a chore when the best part of the game or TV program is on; an elderly parent has become critical, even though extra effort is required to provide his room and board in a nursing home; or God's Word clearly states that a decision is wrong, yet the decision is "right" for the business.

Anger, sarcasm, unjust criticism, unhealthy comparisons, favoritism, inconsistency, jealousy, selfishness, envy, racism, and a host of other ills are "justified" as legal weapons to use against people we consider of little value. Even with our family and loved ones, our anger toward them often comes as a result of something they've done to us that's lowered their value in our eyes.[4] Here's something everyone ought to write on a card and read every day:

> The lower the value we attach to a person, the easier we can "justify" dishonoring them by yelling or treating them with disrespect.

God's Word makes it clear that we're to give honor to Him: "Sing out the honor of His name; Make His praise glorious" (Psalm 66:2).[5] The apostle Paul told us that with other people, including our children, we should "in honor

15

[give] preference to one another'' (Romans 12:10). If we're serious about honoring God, our children, and others, we'll begin to combat our natural bent to dishonor them by taking them lightly. How can we do that? We can begin by understanding two specific aspects of the definition of honor. Each acts as part of the foundation on which the remainder of the book will rest. Each applies first to how we can honor God and then to how we can honor our family and other loved ones. The first aspect of this definition calls us to look on each loved one as a priceless treasure; the other to grant each individual a high place of honor and the loving respect that accompanies it.

A PRICELESS TREASURE

In ancient writings, something of honor was something of substance (literally heavy), valuable, costly, even priceless.[6] For Homer, the Greek scholar, ''The greater the cost of the gift, the more the honor.''[7] The same is often true for biblical authors.[8] David used the word *honor* this way in the psalms, saying, ''How precious [literally, honorable] also are Your thoughts to me, O God!'' (Psalm 139:17). In essence David was saying, ''What a treasure, or how priceless it is, to get to look in on God's thoughts—something believers can do every day in His Word.''

In the New Testament, when Paul wrote to Timothy to encourage believers who were straying into sin, he asked them to be honorable vessels for the Lord—not inexpensive pots of clay that were used for dishonoring purposes, but costly vessels of ''gold and silver'' (2 Timothy 2:20).

For Christians, the greatest example of a priceless treasure is Christ's death on the cross. The apostle Paul certainly recognized this in his writings. When he sternly corrected the Corinthian believers for their immoral lives, he referred to Christ, the priceless sacrifice, to convict them: ''You were bought at a price [literally, with *honor*]; therefore glorify God in your body'' (1 Corinthians 6:20). Every angel and the hosts in heaven recognize the price the

16

Father paid to redeem His people when they sing, "Worthy is the Lamb who was slain / To receive . . . honor!" (Revelation 5:12).

In several places in the Scriptures, the word *honor* actually means "glory."[9] In our relationship with God, honor comes naturally whenever we draw near to Him whose "glory fills the earth" (Psalm 145:5). We can see a picture of how something that is glorious and of great value commands honor in the instructions set forth for His priests and for His tabernacle.

In order to convey the great dignity and importance of the priesthood, the priests' garments, or "royal robes," were designed to be of unusual beauty (Exodus 28:2, 40). From the intricate wood carvings to the priceless ornaments of gold and silver, everything that would stand near God's presence was made with a glorious form (Exodus 35:30–36:1; 40:34).

God isn't impressed by costly robes and priceless vessels, but He knows that we are. Few people can stand next to the Hope diamond, one of the largest diamonds in the world, and not spontaneously be moved by its magnitude, its weight, and the price it commands. When we catch sight of something precious and valuable in creation, our reaction to that treasure gives us an object lesson in how we should respond to God's surpassing glory and beauty.[10]

What does all this have to say to those of us who want to honor our children? One way we honor God is by recognizing that His worth is beyond any price. Similarly, we honor our children by considering them to be special treasures God has entrusted to us.

The Scriptures declare that children are a "gift" from the Lord (Psalm 127:3). They, too, are priceless treasures that we should treat with special care. Why is it so important to look at children as costly gifts or special treasures?

Children Are Gifts of Great Price

Let's be honest. There can be days when that precious little bundle you brought home from the hospital can become a pain in the neck (or someplace farther south). However, as a parent, you can make a decision to treat your child like a valuable treasure. When you do, you raise your positive feelings for that child—even on days when circumstances make all your feelings start out to be negative ones.

At the time we're writing this chapter, it's been six months since my (John's) wife Cindy had a beautiful baby girl. I can't think of a mother who loves her child (or her husband) more, but I also know it isn't always easy. Particularly this past week when combined with Kari's colic, her baby shots, and a stuffy nose cold, she's started teething!

It's times like these when even the most loving parent could be tempted to drop the value of her child. But there's a certain attitude Cindy adopts that steadies her through sleepless nights and equally trying days. Because Cindy makes a daily decision to treasure our daughter, her feelings for Kari rarely drop. How does that work?

Our Lord answers this question in one of our favorite statements: "Where your treasure is, there your heart will be also" (Matthew 6:21). The more you treasure God and His Word, the greater your desire to pray and read His Word. When you learn to treasure your children, your positive feelings for them go up as well.[11]

To get a better handle on what we mean by treasuring someone, try to picture a tangible thing you value. Perhaps it's a new car, an expensive painting, a family heirloom, your father's watch, or a mountain hideaway. For sake of example, let's say you have an expensive, almost priceless painting that's the center of attention in your living room. You would take steps to protect it by making sure it was hung securely and away from direct sunlight; you would highlight it with indirect lighting and a subtle yet elegant frame; you would certainly brag on it to your friends and family because it means so much to you. Because it's of such value, just coming home from work and looking at it could raise your spirits and give you a special feeling inside.

Parents who treasure their children develop many of the same responses. When you treasure a person, you want to protect her; you'll go out of your way to see that she succeeds, and you'll highlight her best points; a valuable loved one would be mentioned frequently in conversations in a positive way. When you place honor on a child, the thought of coming home to her after a long day at work can give you energy, not drain it all away from you.

Isn't it interesting how inanimate objects, such as paintings, tend to keep their value over the years while living objects, such as children, often see their value drop? For parents of toddlers and teen-agers in particular, the decision to treat the children as priceless treasures sometimes has to be made on an hourly basis! But it pays rich dividends.

Children are incredibly perceptive. When it looks as if you value the house, job, car, or pet poodle more than them, your actions speak far louder than your words. In the chapters that follow, we'll look at a number of ways you can actively communicate to your children that they are treasures to you.

A HIGHLY RESPECTED POSITION

There's a second meaning of the word *honor* that can help us understand how it builds value into our loved ones. Not only does it signify something or someone who is a priceless treasure, but it is also used for someone who occupies a highly respected position in our lives, someone high on our priority list.[12]

In ancient Greece, the word *honor* was reserved for "men who are in a high position."[13] It was used to designate a king or those of his inner circle. Later it came to apply to anyone who deserved special mention for the place he held in someone's life.[14]

In the Scriptures, the classic example is Christ. Because of His sacrifice and because of His calling, He takes the place of honor as our High Priest before the Father.[15] The more we understand about the place He holds with the Father, the greater our respect for who He is and what He continues to accomplish in and through us.

For the Greeks, giving people honor because of the positions they held or what they had accomplished was inseparable from treating them with respect. The very word *respect* means "to look behind."[16] In other words, it involves looking back and seeing a person's accomplishments, then treating him as very valuable.

One way we honor God today is to look back on all He has done for us. That's why the writers of the psalms call on us so often to "remember."[17] One way we honor our loved ones, parents, and family members is to give them a high position on our priority list and look back in thanks on how they've enriched our lives.

But what if you look back at your parents or other loved ones and find that they *don't* deserve your thanks? For example, what if through ignorance or through a lack of caring, your parents failed to provide you with the actions or memories that deserve your respect? What if they used their position in your life for harm rather than good?

Like counting someone as a valuable treasure, granting a person respect is a decision you have to make. Emotionally, you may or may not "feel" like giving honor to your parents, but you can still make a decision to do so.

One way we honor our loved ones, parents, and family members is to give them a high position on our priority list and look back in thanks on how they've enriched our lives.

We know that some mothers and fathers haven't earned the right to be honored. But we also know that the highest form of love bestows honor on someone who doesn't deserve it. And as we'll show, *the only way to achieve real freedom from the effects of a dishonoring parent is to honor that person.*

What place do your children feel they have in your life? Some parents really don't want their children to answer this question. Hearing a child say he feels as though he's fifth place in your life can be a crushing blow, as it was for Walter.

Walter was a pastor who heard us describe what it meant to honor a person, and he went home and asked his son what kind of position he felt he occupied in his father's life.

"Do you really want to know?" asked his teen-aged son.

"Certainly," his dad replied.

"All my life, I've felt like it's been ministry, ministry, ministry, ministry, family, and then ministry."

When children grow up feeling low on their parents' list of priorities, major problems can result. Many children will spend a lifetime languishing in an emotional cubbyhole from being "low-listed"—afraid and unwilling to break out of it.

Thankfully, many parents take steps to make sure that children occupy a place of significance in the home. The knowledge that they rate high on their mother and father's list can be, in and of itself, a tremendous boost to their feeling valuable and significant.

APPLYING HONOR IN OUR HOMES

Thus far we've looked at the biblical concept of honor from three different angles and seen three clear reflections from the literal meaning of this word (and its opposite) that can guide us throughout the book. But how do we apply this to our loved ones, especially our children? How does this knowledge help us raise their self-worth and battle any feeling of inferiority they may have?

The pages that follow focus on seven ways parents can practically apply honor in their most important relationships and see their children's feeling of value raised as a result.

We're excited to help you discover (or be reminded of) what we've seen make a tremendous difference in families across the country, including our own. We want you to walk with us through the next few pages as we give you a thumbnail sketch of the various ways you'll be able to help your own children to honor God and others and feel of great value themselves. Throughout this book as you understand and apply each principle, you'll be **giving the gift of honor when your children see you . . .**

Extending It First to Your Own Parents

Many of us do not realize that when we dishonor our parents, we not only hurt them but also rob ourselves of a sense of value and fail to pass down value and acceptance to our own children. Not only that, we give our children a model and an excuse for dishonoring us and repeating a negative cycle generation after generation.

Punching holes in our parents drains away our physical, spiritual, and emotional energy. And the less worth and energy we have ourselves, the less we have to pass along to our children.

Helping Them Find Value in Troubled Times

In looking at this aspect of honoring our children, we'll be tackling one of the most frequently asked questions in counseling and at conferences: "How do I help my child work through some of the most discouraging and damaging experiences he or she faces?"

Many moms and dads are afraid of what their children might experience in life, but few of them are equipped to help their children through major difficulties should they actually occur. While it is our hope that neither our readers nor their children will ever go through tragedies, the Scriptures tell us various trials will come (James 1). What then?

We can learn a method of walking our children (or ourselves) through discouraging, even devastating experiences that would ordinarily lower their sense of self-respect or value. These same negative experiences can then be used to increase their feelings of worth. Parents can even begin to see their own sense of anxiety lowered as they learn how to face the very experience most people only know how to avoid.

Recognizing Your Parenting Strengths and Style

Why are some parents stricter than others? Why do some children leave home seemingly secure and confident and others do not? Why does one parent seem assured while the parent next door suffers great insecurities?

At least in part, the answers to these questions lie in the different parenting strengths and styles men and women possess. In these sections, we want to help you discover your primary parenting strengths and how God can use these natural gifts to build value into your children. We also want to help you see how each parenting style can build up a child's sense of value or, if pushed to an extreme, break it down.

Providing a Healthy Balance in Your Home

Another important question that often surfaces when we talk with parents is some variation of this theme: "How do we know how to balance staying close to our children yet releasing them to develop healthy independence?"

We deal with this question by illustrating a healthy balance, a biblical balance, between "belonging" and "separateness" necessary in each family's home. Specifically, we'll share ways parents can help their children feel the warmth of belonging, as well as ease them into independence. We'll also highlight what happens to children who grow up in out-of-balance homes, where they are forced to live at either extreme.

Establishing Loving Boundaries for Them

Throughout the Scriptures and in numerous current studies, we are told that providing loving limits for our children helps raise their value and sense of self-worth. Each time we make the effort to provide a loving boundary for our children, we not only protect them but help to produce security and confidence in their lives.

Providing protective fences for our children and learning how to maintain them is one of the most important ways we can encourage our sons and daughters. Loving boundaries can also help a child answer four crucial questions every person needs to answer to combat temptation and truly feel valuable.

Building Positive Loyalties into Them

In every home, invisible lines of loyalty stretch across thousands of miles and through decades of time. Even adults who have long since moved away from home can still stumble daily over these cords from the past.

Because of the nature of children, every home and every parent builds lines of loyalty into a child. There is little debate over the fact that children repeat patterns they see in their parents. What remains a toss-up is whether the patterns they adopt will be positive or negative when they become adults.

Every day we are laying down lines of loyalty for our children. To make sure these patterns are positive, we'll focus on the way God establishes positive loyalties with His children through His "loyal-love," including several specific patterns we can adopt in building value into our children.

Offering Honor to God

Finally, in this section, we see that the same elements that help us build value into our children can also help them raise their value of God! As we discover ways we can teach our children to honor God, we will also learn a major reason why many of us have such a difficult time reading God's Word or spending time in prayer. These are lessons which we can pass along to our children to help them have a more consistent spiritual life.

Seven aspects of honor, each with the power to make a major positive difference in our child's life if applied. However, before we as parents are truly free to build a sense of value into our children, we must first understand why honoring our own parents or their memory is so important. The decision we make in this area can either leave us stuck on a muddy road or well on the highway toward giving honor to our loved ones.

CHAPTER THREE

Extending the Gift First to Our Own Parents

Tami was thirty-two years old when she realized that most of her shattered relationships could be tied directly to her lifelong struggle with her father. Emotionally, she had been fighting him and her painful past for years, and her energy and joy in the present had been drained away.

He hadn't been the best of fathers, and for years she took every opportunity she could to remind him of that fact. Twice she married men just like him; twice she ended those marriages in frustration and bitterness.

What made Tami feel a need for counseling was the way her children were beginning to act toward her. She never wanted to see her family go through the same kind of struggles she had, but when she took an honest look at what her children were experiencing, she saw a mirror reflection of her own life as a child.

One of the first things Tami learned in counseling was also one of the most difficult things she had to do. Even though she understood how much it would help her, she was only willing to accept it when she understood how much it would benefit her children.

What did Tami have to face? As a parent who wanted to honor her children by building value into their lives, she had to begin by becoming aware of the need to honor her own mom and dad. By attaching significance and worth to her parents, she would benefit personally, and she would model for her children how they should act toward her.

As much as some people would like to ignore this fact, the Scriptures make it clear that one of the first steps on the road to honoring others begins with honoring "your father and your mother, . . . that your days may be long, and that it may be well with you" (Deuteronomy 5:16). Why is this so important? Some individuals may live thousands of miles from their parents. Others may not have thought of them for years. Still others, whose parents are deceased, may be able to deal with them only through memories (which can be just as vivid, or more so, than life).

In the pages that follow, we'll look at four reasons why it's crucial for us not to short-circuit God's command to honor our parents. But before we address this issue, there's something we need to highlight, particularly for those who grew up in a less-than-ideal home situation.

WHAT? HONOR *MY* PARENTS?

We're sure that there will be individuals who read this book (perhaps even you) and bristle with anger at the mere suggestion of giving honor to parents. "Honor *my* parents? After what my father did to me? After all I had to go through with my mother? Are you kidding? Give me a break!"

Without a doubt, there are some parents whose insensitivity and unloving actions have hurt their children deeply. We know well that some mothers and fathers don't appear to deserve honor. We're not saying their actions weren't hurtful, nor are we explaining away the negative effects they may have had over the years. However, we are saying that the only way to be free from the hurt they have caused you is to honor them. In short, *continuing to nail your parents to a cross years after the fact* **hurts** *you more than it does them.*

Most of us grew up with loving parents who tried their

best to build value into our lives. For those of you who did not, the next chapter is directed toward you. There we'll show how the trials you suffered at the hands of a dishonoring parent (or anyone else for that matter) can be used to bring positive gain into your life. But for now, let's look at four reasons each of us has for honoring our parents, whether or not they're alive today.

REJECTING OUR PARENTS IS ROBBING FROM OURSELVES

Brad didn't hate his father, but he didn't like him either. His father had always been very demanding of him as a child, and for years Brad continued to resent it. Perhaps that's why he said so often to his wife and children (and anyone else who would listen) that he had little respect for his dad.

Invariably, as Brad would be watching a television show and a villainous character would come on, he would make some wisecrack about his father. Whenever he did something special for his children, he would always preface it with the remark, "You wouldn't find *my* dad doing something like this with *his* kids."

Long before they ever met him, the children had a vivid image of their grandfather. On a good day, they knew he must be a cross between Attila the Hun and Archie Bunker. The very first time David, Brad's five-year-old son, met his grandfather, he walked up to him, doubled up his fist, and took a swing at him!

In some ways, it made Brad feel better to put down his dad. When he was growing up, he never had anyone to talk over his frustrations with, and as an adult, he felt justified in getting them all off his chest. What Brad didn't realize (and what other "Brads" and "Bettys" often aren't aware of) was that *every time he dishonored his father, he was lowering his own self-worth.* How does this happen?

All of us are very much like our parents and very much a part of them. We pick up many of their emotional charac-

27

teristics and bents, and our physical bodies are forever marked by them, too. Chromosomes are God's building blocks for our physical development, and at conception, half of them came from each parent. From that one fact alone, it should be obvious that we can never escape our parents. Each of our cells bears the vestiges of their stamp on our lives.

When God tells us to honor our parents, it's with good reason. When we lower their value and cut them down, we're dishonoring a part of ourselves. Brad was doing even more.

When Brad's children met their grandfather, they were surprised by two things. First, he didn't seem as big as they thought he would be. Second, he acted so much like their father!

It causes incredible confusion in a child's mind when he's been taught to dislike characteristics in his grandparents that he sees every day in his own mom or dad. Like a marksman firing off a scatter-gun at close range, a child who blasts out at his grandfather knows he will hit his father as well.

For years, Brad didn't realize the harm he was doing to himself. The more he dishonored his father, the lower his own sense of self-worth sank. The lower his worth, the more difficult he became to live with and the harder he was on his children and wife.

It bears repeating that people with low self-worth tend to act out their feelings of anger and inadequacy. If their feeling of dislike for themselves is deep enough, they often strain every relationship and get other people to treat them in the negative way they feel about themselves. People with low self-worth aren't easy to live with, and that was certainly true of Brad.

Brad tried all his life to get away from the hurtful memory of his father, but by dishonoring him, he ended up staring at him every morning in the mirror. His children knew it, too. Brad hated the way he had been treated by his father, and his children knew exactly how he felt because it was exactly the way Brad treated them.

As we have seen, making the decision not to honor our parents gives our sons and daughters their first lesson in how to dishonor us. And just as in Brad's case, the lack of joy and the shortened life we get out of dishonoring them[1] keep us from being able to love our children as we should.

Besides draining away our capacity to love others, dishonoring our parents does something else. It builds a wall around relationships that can block us from truly developing our masculinity or femininity.

IN SEARCH OF MASCULINITY AND FEMININITY

For any child, his first look at masculinity comes from observing his father, and his first look at femininity from observing his mother. What happens when a child cuts himself off from his parents? Pushed to an extreme, it can edge a person toward homosexuality.

Although many factors are involved, much current research on homosexual behavior is centered on boys who were cut off, emotionally or physically, from their fathers.[2] When a male child grows up disliking and avoiding his father, he also runs the risk of being blocked from identifying with his maleness. All too often, an overly involved mother comes into the picture with a son who is being shunned or not accepted by his father, and she is all too willing to pick up the slack. Because of an uninvolved or uncaring father, the mother-son attachment can grow incredibly strong.

In extreme cases, young boys identify almost totally with their mother and her actions, yet they remain in search of an idealized "someone" to replace their absent father. Such boys and young men are easy prey for a homosexual encounter.

While homosexuality may represent the extreme of being unable to identify with a father, dishonoring our parents can affect each of us in more subtle ways.

Recently, we met a middle-aged woman named Dayna who grew up in a dishonoring home. For years, even after she became a Christian, she hated her father with a passion. His continual drinking and lack of support for the household required her mother to work full-time and kept Dayna from having any of her friends visit her at home. By the time she was old enough to marry and move out of the house, her anger toward her father—and toward men in general—had been honed to a razor's edge.

Dayna's first marriage lasted two years—two years of constant criticism and fighting after she discovered on their honeymoon that her husband's social drinking was much more than that. Her second marriage had lasted years longer, but she was unable to be satisfactorily intimate with her husband.

When we saw this couple in counseling and suggested that the way she continually dishonored her father had a role in her marriage problems, she became so upset that she got up and walked out of the room. Only after several weeks of her husband's pleading was she willing to come back for another session.

In no way were her father's actions justified. They caused hurt for her mother and incredible pain for her. His sin was wrong, and he stands accountable for it to the Lord. But twenty years later, it wasn't her father who was continuing to suffer, it was Dayna.

By refusing to forgive him, she chained herself to the very person she wanted so desperately to avoid. By doggedly holding on to hurts in the past, she moved further and further away from enjoying life in the present.

Dayna's inability to identify with the most powerful masculine figure in her life, her father, also contributed to the continual struggle she had with every other man who tried to get close to her, including the men she married.[3] Listen to what she told us near the end of our time of counseling:

> Deep down inside, all my life I have thought that men were nothing but sleazeballs. I couldn't even enjoy my husband holding me because he reminded me so much of my father. I even resented the fact that God gave me two boys and no girls.
>
> I want to be close to my husband and my children, and I want to be close to God. But I know because I view them as men I don't really trust them.

And therein lies one of the worst effects of dishonoring her dad. It's bad enough that it can cut her off from forming a close attachment to her spouse or her children, but it's even worse that it can block her from a fulfilling relationship with the heavenly Father, especially His masculine side.[4]

Similar problems can result if someone cuts herself off from the most powerful feminine figure in her life, her mother. If she dishonors her, watch how few nurturing qualities, how few relationship skills, and how little sensitivity develop in her life.

Not being able to identify with a difficult, uncaring mother was the very thing that led a young woman named Marian to become every inch a "man" by her dress and actions. Deep inside, Marian became so angry with her mother, who presented a very feminine side to people, that she wanted nothing to do with dresses or make-up or anything that made her look more like her mother. She managed to look very different from her mother on the outside, yet she acted just as controlling, angry, and manipulative on the inside.

Besides lowering our value and threatening to cut us off from significant relationships with other men or women, and even with God, there's a third negative result of dishonoring our parents. According to the Scriptures, we pay a terrible *physical* price for lowering our parents' worth.

THE PHYSICAL EFFECTS OF DISHONORING MOM AND DAD

Some people refused to quit smoking until the surgeon general came out with his warning labels and long list of physical ailments linked to cigarettes. Although we don't pretend to be surgeons, we've come across some interesting studies that we hope might help people stop treating their parents with as little value as a light mist.

In God's first commandment with a promise, "Honor your father and your mother,"[5] you can't get away from the physical side effects that come from agreeing with or tossing aside God's Word. Either your life will be lengthened and your days brightened, or you run the risk of shortening your life and darkening your days.

In a simplified way, we'd like to share with you one reason

31

why dishonoring mom and dad does such physical damage.[6] It all begins inside the brain, where the decision you make to harbor negative feelings toward your parents can set off a series of physical events you would do well to avoid.

To better understand this concept, try to think in terms of an outer brain and an inner brain. The outer brain, basically located in the outer cortex, acts like the programmer, the person who punches the raw data into a computer. He gathers all the incoming information from each of the five senses, makes a decision on it, and sends the equation that matches the decision down to the inner brain.

The inner brain acts like the computer itself. Once it receives the equation, it follows the instructions to the letter. The inner brain doesn't worry about making the right decision. It simply responds to what it has been commanded to do.[7]

Let's see how this applies to honoring or dishonoring parents by going back to the story of Brad. He had real problems with his father, and dishonoring him had become almost second nature. What Brad didn't realize was that every time he made a decision (outer brain) to dishonor his father, chemicals were being released into his body (by the inner brain) that could shorten his life. To understand how this happens, we need to know more about how the brain functions.

Let's say a man is out jogging one afternoon when a neighbor's large dog starts to run toward him. Instantly, the jogger's outer brain kicks into action to make a decision about what to do.

For example, his outer brain might be saying, "Okay, my eyes tell me there's a dog running at me. It's a big dog. In fact, it's one of the *biggest* dogs I've ever seen! He doesn't look all that friendly either. In fact, his hair is standing straight up! If I try to outrun him, he'll jump on me and eat me alive! This isn't a good situation. I mean, I'm really in trouble! I know I can't outrun him, so I think I'd better stop, stand still, and hope for the best."[8]

Once a decision has been made in the outer brain, it's transferred down to the inner brain. The inner brain reads the instructions it's handed and relays its instructions verbatim to the many important glands it controls. If we could listen in, we might hear something like this:

"Okay down there! Listen up quick! Let's release a bunch of adrenalin to get our heart moving quicker. Double the blood pressure! Lungs, you'll have to move oxygen in and out faster to keep pace! Pituitary gland! Work on increasing the sugar content in our system, and while you're at it, make it easier for our blood to clot just in case the dog decides to bite. To be safe, it says here in the instructions we need to dilate those pupils so we can see the dog better. And for right now all digestion and elimination is to come to a halt. Got it? Good, you've only got about two seconds to get everything ready before the dog gets here."

Our jogger has made a decision (outer brain) about a stressful event, and his body responds (inner brain) dramatically to that decision. Let's say that in this case the dog happens to be a big, lovable animal who is lonely for some company. He runs over to the man, stands up and puts his paws on the jogger's shoulders, and licks him in the face.

Petting the dog for a few moments and slowly moving along his way, the jogger suddenly feels faint and starts to shake. That's the natural result of his body's trying to get back to normal after all those chemicals were dumped into his blood stream. Even once the threat has been reduced to a nonthreatening, playful dog (even a big one), it takes the body quite a while to get everything back to normal!

Staying on the Alert Too Long

How does all this concern Brad and his decision to dishonor his father? Just suppose that last night Brad was watching a rerun of "Little House on the Prairie," and he got steaming mad at the controlling, manipulative Mrs. Olsen. Then he started thinking about how manipulative and controlling his own father was while he was growing up, and he got even angrier. As though that wasn't enough, just before bedtime he remembered that his father was coming the next day for one of his obligatory visits, and oooh, he didn't want to see him.

Understanding what's happening inside Brad's brain at this point gives us at least one illustration of how our lives can be shortened. If Brad realized this, perhaps he would understand why he's been having such a hard time falling asleep at night and why, when he awakens, his stomach is churning and his jaws are sore from grinding his teeth. With all the stress Brad puts on his body each year, it's no wonder he gets the flu or a cold so often that everyone at the doctor's office calls him by his first name.

When Brad makes a decision that his father is worthless, a pain in the neck, or nothing but trouble, his body goes on the alert. When the inner brain gets the message that there's a stressful situation out there (in this case a "bad dad"), it doesn't ask questions—it just reacts. Brad's body can easily release as many chemicals and disrupt as many bodily functions when he is angry with his father as it would if he were being chased by his neighbor's dog.

What happens when our bodies stay on the alert too long? Undesirable things such as clinical depression, colitis, bleeding ulcers, anxiety attacks, lowered resistance to colds and flu, heart and respiratory failure.[9] Some researchers believe that cancer can and does take place.[10] Such stress on our bodies can shorten our lives on this earth; thus the negative promise in God's Word may be fulfilled.

If you haven't been challenged to answer the question yet, let's ask it pointblank: To what degree are you dishonoring your parents today? For any of us who are majoring in lowering our parents' value, at the same time we're **minoring in lowering** our own self-worth and that of our children, risking cutting ourselves off from intimate relationships with other men, women, and God Himself, and physically damaging our bodies. As if this isn't enough, there's more!

THE DARKNESS FROM DISHONORING OUR PARENTS

There's a fourth reason why we need to honor our parents. Actually, it should be reason enough, in and of itself. God commands us to do so: "Honor your father and mother . . . that it may be well with you and you may live long on the earth" (Ephesians 6:2–3).

In the psalms, we're told that God's Word is a light to our paths and a lamp to our feet.[11] When we decide to ignore His Word, we walk away from the light and into the darkness. Our loving heavenly Father knew the pain we would have if we stumbled around in the dark so He provided His Word as a clear light for our paths.

None of us can afford to forget the truth that persistent anger directed toward anyone leads us right into darkness (1 John 2:9ff.). Darkness keeps us from knowing or walking in the light of God's path. Making a decision to honor our parents, even if we have to call on God for the strength to do so, keeps us out of darkness and our children from learning a negative pattern.

There may be times when the path God's Word illuminates is not the same one we want to take—like the road that leads to honoring our parents—but a loving God knows it will be far worse for us in many ways to experience the illegitimate pain of falling in darkness than to face the legitimate pain of dealing with our past in the light.

HOW DO WE GIVE HONOR TO OUR PARENTS?

Honoring our parents follows the pattern we have described earlier in the book: making a decision to treat them (or their memory) as a valuable treasure, and granting them a position of high respect in our lives. However, before we look at specific ways in which we can do this, we need to evaluate how highly we're valuing them today.

Evaluate Current Attitudes and Actions

Assessing our current attitudes and actions toward our parents is particularly important for those people who may have kept their parents at arms' length as a way of dealing with past hurts. If you recall from chapter 2, the picture the Scripture gives of dishonoring someone is treating him like an insignificant mist. Each of us needs to ask, "Do I brush my mother and father aside, or do I count them as weighty and valuable?''

Jim would never have thought or admitted that he was dishonoring his father, but he was. Jim's mother and father had divorced when he was very young, and it wasn't until his early teens that he and his father re-established contact. For Jim, however, now that the years had passed and he had a family of his own, spending time with his father or checking in with him occasionally was something he continually put off.

Anger didn't bubble over on the surface when he did see his father, but it was always lying just beneath the surface. Their conversation was usually shallow when they got together, filled with talk of sports or the weather. Instead of bringing up the tension that had dominated their relationship for years, they walked around issues that desperately needed confronting as carefully as if they were walking through a minefield.

Jim was not openly dishonoring his father, but his ignoring him for months on end was a subtle way to accomplish the same thing. Instead of facing the hard issues and working through them himself or with his father, he let silence and procrastination shut out his unhappiness.

Jim's case isn't unusual. Even when there hasn't been a major family fracture, many people who live within an hour of their parents only contact them on a yearly basis.

When you ignore your parents, even when you're busy with your own lives and family, you dishonor them. You don't have to call them four times a day or invite them on every vacation, but putting off making contact with them as a subtle form of punishment or insensitivity dishonors them.

How can you combat the tendency to slip parents beyond the back burner? Let's look at some practical ways of applying the twofold instructions of our definition of honor.

Take Time to "Look Back"

Attitudes influence actions, and that is particularly true when it comes to your parents. If you place your present view of your parents on a value line, perhaps you can determine how much you treasure them. On a line marked off from 1 to 10, if 10 means high value and 1 means low, where would you put your present value of your parents?

My Present View of My Parents

1	2	3	4	5	6	7	8	9	10
Little value								High value	

The reason many of us fail to call or write our parents is that their present value in our busy lives is probably at a 4 or below. Remember the principle we gave earlier: What you treasure is what you'll have good feelings for.[12] If your parents are near the bottom of your value line, you may not feel like contacting them or expressing any thanks for what they've done in your life. But if you make a decision to move up their value, your feelings for them may move up as well.

Biblical Instructions on Honoring Our Parents

1. It honors our parents to listen carefully to their counsel. (Proverbs 1:8, 2:1, 3:1, 4:1, 5:1, 9:8, 10:1, 13:1, and 15:5)
2. It honors our parents when they see their children acting wisely. (Proverb 27:11)
3. Sharing "good news" with our parents can bring "health to their bones." (Proverb 15:30)
4. Praising our parents brings light to our lives; cursing them will snuff out our lamp. (Proverb 20:20)
5. It dishonors ourselves and our parents when we act foolishly. (Proverb 17:25)
6. Involvement in immoral relationships not only affects us, but also causes our parents to grieve and lose their energy. (Proverbs 5:1ff, 31:3)
7. Pride and a "haughty spirit," saying we're "pure" when we're not, expressing critical and judgmental words like a "mouth full of knives," and mocking our mother and father bring dishonor to a parent. (Proverbs 30:12–17)

The Scriptures say that the wise man honors his mother and father, and the fool ignores and hates them (Proverb 30:17). Making a decision to treat them as special treasures can be one of the wisest things you ever do.

The second aspect of the definition of honor can help to accomplish the first. The way to treasure your parents is by "looking back" at them with respect. In the previous chapter, you saw that to respect a person literally means to "look back." But very few people develop the honoring habit of "looking back." In Jesus' day, in one instance it was only one out of ten. Do you remember the story in the New Testament about Christ's healing ten lepers? (Luke 17:11–19). That was no small feat or act of love. These lepers were tremendously needy, and Jesus met their deepest physical needs. But how many turned back? One! Only one man out of ten who could have stopped to express thanks and appreciation, bothered to do so.

As we look around, we still see as few as one in ten taking the time to look back and say thanks to their parents. But practically, how can we do that? First, let's look at a list from the Scriptures that can give us insight into what honors and what dishonors our parents.

Below are responses from parents of various ages who were asked the question "What could your children do or have they done to make you feel honored?"

What Could My Children Do to Honor Me?

1. *On a day other than Mother or Father's Day, it would mean so much to get a card or letter from our children letting us know they're thinking of us.*
2. *The greatest present I ever received from my son was a cassette tape that looked back on several specific things I had done for him in the past.*
3. *Even though it's difficult for me to do, my daughter always makes a point of hugging me when we get together.*
4. *As a single mom, when my (school-age) children do chores without being asked, or additional chores, I feel honored.*

5. *It honors me to see my children reaching out to help others who have been less fortunate than they.*

6. *I feel flattered and humbled when my daughter asks my advice on struggles and needs in her life.*

7. *We appreciate the way our children tell us the truth, even when it means disagreeing with us or expressing an opinion different from ours.*

8. *We know our children are praying for us every day and that honors us.*

9. *When I see my daughter seeking after God, I can't think of anything that brings me more honor.*

10. *When my children were in their teen-age years, they came to us to talk about "taboo" areas like drinking, sex, and drugs.*

11. *My son and I have often disagreed over the years, but it means so much that we've cleared up past hurts.*

12. *Receiving a special thank you after we've babysat the grandchildren is a real encouragement.*

13. *I think the greatest way my daughter honored me was to name her daughter after me.*

14. *When I see my (school-age) children do their best in school or on different projects, it honors me.*

15. *A while ago, I learned from a neighbor that my son had praised me and actually defended me in front of several people when I wasn't present.*

16. *My son's admitting he was wrong in the way he was treating his wife and agreeing to get marriage counseling was something for which I'll always be thankful.*

17. *When my children let me spend time with the grandchildren, I feel honored.*

18. *Although he knew he didn't have to, my nineteen-year-old son helped out by paying some of the grocery and rent costs when we were having a tough time making ends meet.*

19. *At my husband's funeral, I cried when my two sons and one daughter came up to me and told me they would love and take care of me as I grew older.*

20. *Watching the way my son treats his wife and children, and then hearing him say he learned it from us, is something that is more valuable than any present he could give me.*

(In *The Blessing,* look at the chapter "Giving the Blessing to Your Parents" for other suggestions.)[13]

We know there will be people who read these comments and respond by saying, "If my parents had done some of those things for me, maybe I would take the time to honor them!" Out of anger over the message of this chapter, you are certainly free to skip this section, read ahead, and put into practice the other aspects of honor we offer in this book. But you will never see the short- or long-term effects on your life or your children's lives if you do.

How can you learn to honor a dishonoring parent? How can you stop chasing past hurts and be at peace in the present? At the beginning of the chapter, we promised we would speak to the special needs of those of you who came from deeply dishonoring homes—people who may still be saying, "There's no way I could ever respect my parents, you've never met them!"

In the next chapter, we'll look at how negative events can bring some of the most positive effects to our lives. But for now, let's meet a man named Jerry, who never believed anything positive could come from his relationship with his parents, especially his devastating relationship with his father. Although he would never have considered it at one point in his life, Jerry was free from the hurts in his past only when he learned to honor his father and find value in trials.

COULD ANYTHING GOOD COME FROM JERRY'S HOME?

Jerry was plagued with feelings of worthlessness and discouragement most of his life. These feelings also made it difficult for him to receive love from his wife or to give love to her and their children. Where did such negative feelings begin? Just like many other "Jerrys" we've met—in a dishonoring home.

Jerry's father was a deacon in the church, and the family spent a lot of time at church. But if someone had peeled away the thin veneer of happiness and spirituality that greeted outsiders, he would have seen a terrible problem eating away at this family from within. Because Jerry's father had begun to question God's Word on right and wrong and on what makes healthy relationships, this "model" family was beginning to deteriorate.

Children, even very young children, are incredibly perceptive about picking up signs of strain in their parents' marriage, and Jerry knew his parents were struggling in theirs. Increasingly, his mother and father would ride separately to church and sit with other people when they got there. Also, at least in front of the children, they had quit touching or hugging each other. As a twelve-year-old boy, Jerry was concerned about his parents' marriage. Yet what hurt him the most was the knowledge that, for whatever reason, he no longer lived up to his dad's expectations.

Jerry could see this firsthand every Sunday after church as he sat at the dinner table with another boy his age whom he could tell his father idolized. Jerry's mother had a close friend who would come over after church and bring her teen-age son, Don. For Jerry, it was the hardest time of the week. He had to listen to his father say things to another boy that he longed for his father to say to him. Jerry's father never seemed to run out of questions about Don's week at school or praise for the way he had played in his latest football or baseball game. And every time Jerry's father put Don up on a pedestal, he lowered his own son's value.

Occasionally, when his father's rapt attention would become too obvious, Jerry's mother would shift the conversation and ask something about Jerry's week. But from the look his father gave him and the way the conversation would invariably swing back to Don, it was all too clear that his father wasn't interested in or impressed with anything he was involved in.

41

The way his father *looked* at the other boy tore holes in his heart. While Jerry would hardly receive a glance, his father's eyes would brighten and his face would soften at the very sight of Don.

By now, you've guessed that Jerry's father had his value system out of whack, but he couldn't (or wouldn't) see it. As a result, what should have been of utmost worth to him, his relationship with the Lord and his family, became of little value.

One mark of mental health is that people can differentiate between what is truly valuable and what is of little worth. The roots of mental illness can be reflected by people such as addicts who view drugs as being more valuable than the person's possessions he steals or the workaholic who trades in his relationship with his family for a minor promotion. *When people begin a habitual pattern of dishonoring others, they are only a few steps away from trading in the permanent for the immediate.*[14]

For months, Jerry endured this torturous Sunday lunchtime ritual. Then one day it happened. On a school night, Jerry's mother came up the stairs and gently knocked at his door. She sat down on his bed, and at first all she could do was put her head in her hands and weep. Finally, through broken words, she told Jerry that she and his father were divorcing. And then she told him the rest of the story. *Jerry's father was going to marry Don's mother!*

The ultimate way to dishonor another person in marriage—divorce—will happen hundreds of thousands of times this year alone.[15] The tearing apart of what God has meant to last a lifetime invariably results in a husband and wife deeply devaluing each other, and it greatly affects the children as well. Anger, lowered self-worth, guilt, fear, and even a high suicide rate are found among those experiencing the trauma of divorce.[16]

In the more than twenty years since Jerry's parents divorced, he has seen his father only one time. That was when he found out from his uncle that his father would be flying through his hometown and would have a two-hour layover between flights. He called his dad and asked if he could see him at the airport.

The Death of a Dream

Jerry was filled with expectation. He took along pictures of his children his father had never met and even a copy of an article he had written for a Christian magazine. He thought about all the things he wanted to share with his dad, but he never got the chance. From the time they met at the gate until only a few minutes were left before he had to leave, Jerry's father talked on and on about what Don and his family were doing.

When he could stand it no longer, Jerry broke in and asked his father, "Don't you want to know what's been happening in *my* life?"

His father stopped and looked down at his shoes. "Jerry," his father said slowly as he looked up, "I'm sure whatever you're doing is going very well."

Those were the last words the two men spoke to each other. A heavy silence hung over them until the call came from the reservation desk announcing his father's flight. After his dad left, Jerry walked out to his car, buried his head in his arms, and cried—heart-rending sobs that come only when you know you've seen a loved one for the last time.

Jerry's father has never visited Jerry's home, but his ghost haunts every room. Two times in the past five years, Jerry has sent a letter to his father. Neither time has he received an answer.

Jerry's father made a decision years ago. He started walking away from God's Word, and as a result, he began dishonoring it and other people. The same thing is true of anyone who puts aside God's Word and begins walking in darkness.

Jerry and his mother were treated as people with little value or worth. As a result, it has left a legacy of hurt feelings and emotional pain that they continue to wear like a heavy pinecone wreath. It's uncomfortable and constantly pricks at them (especially on anniversaries, birthdays, and holidays), and it keeps them from letting others get close enough to wound them again. In Jerry's case, that has included keeping his own wife and children at arm's length.

As we pause here, perhaps you're wondering how anything good could come out of a story like this. With all the rejection this man has felt over the years, and still experiences today, what possible benefit could come from all his trials? How could such treatment lead to anything but low worth and the problems associated with it?

The next chapter provides some answers. Jerry looked back, faced his past, and made a decision to give his father honor. He developed the ability to treasure his father as a valuable person in spite of the way he had been treated. You'll see how he turned the terrible experience with his dad into higher self-worth and how even his own family benefitted from what he learned.

The same things Jerry learned can help us all deal with difficulties and heartache in our lives and teach us how our children can learn to respond to suffering in a way that honors God and themselves. Teaching our children to find value in trials is the next vital step in honoring them and building value into their lives.

CHAPTER FOUR

Helping Our Children Find Value in Troubled Times: Part 1

It was early evening when Mary's mother walked by her daughter's room on the way to the kitchen. An active junior in high school, Mary rarely stayed home on a Friday night. Perhaps that was why her mother stopped outside her door for a moment and listened.

She couldn't be sure, but she thought she heard muffled crying. As she gently knocked on her daughter's door, it opened a few inches, and she could see her daughter lying on the bed with her head buried in a pillow.

"Mary? What's wrong, honey?"

"Nothing," Mary replied as she sat up quickly, trying to stifle the emotion in her voice and pull herself together. "Nothing's wrong."

Her mother opened the door, walked over to the bed, and sat down beside her. "Mary, you know you can tell me if something is wrong. Your dad and I love you very much, and we're here for you if you need us."

Unable to control her emotions, Mary laid her head in her mother's lap and sobbed uncontrollably. "I'm so sorry, Mom. I'm so sorry . . . I just can't believe it . . . I just can't believe it happened to me."

After letting her daughter cry for some time, Mary's mother finally urged her to sit up. "Honey, don't you think you'd better tell me what's bothering you?"

Looking down at her hands, in a voice that sounded

foreign even to herself, Mary choked out the words, "Mom . . . I'm pregnant. I went to a doctor and had the test done, and it was positive."

Looking up at her mother, Mary began to cry again. "How am I going to tell Dad? What do I do about school and my friends? Oh, Mom, what am I going to do?"

WHEN TRIALS CRASH INTO OUR CHILDREN'S LIVES

For most parents, these words would represent one of the greatest tragedies their child could face. About to begin college or a career, the child sees lifelong dreams and hopes suddenly go up in smoke. In their place stand the cold, harsh realities of an unplanned pregnancy and the emotional scars that often result.

As parents, we may never have to experience the pain that comes from children caught up in immorality, but our children will experience many types of trials. The Scriptures assure us of that.[1] Trials and difficult times are unavoidable. Although we may work overtime trying to protect our children from pain, we'll never be able to isolate them totally from being hurt by their own or by others' actions.

As loving parents, one way we can honor our children and build value into their lives is to help them see the positive gain in troubled times. Whether we like it or not, before they leave our homes, our sons or daughters may experience moments or even days of doubt, discouragement, loneliness, disappointment, or depression.

They may be betrayed by a friend, fail to get into the college or the profession of their choice, be dumped later in life by a spouse, or perhaps experience the disabling results of experimenting with drugs or alcohol. And with each painful experience their child suffers, Mom and Dad feel the aftershocks in their hearts.

If a child doesn't know how to deal with trials in a positive way, he stands a great chance of being emotionally and spiritually handicapped, and his relationships later in life can suffer. Whether he's stuck with fears and anxiety or saddled with deepening bitterness and resentment, he can have a difficult time trying to cope with his negative experiences, and his lowered self-worth can adversely affect his emotional development.

This is exactly what happened to Jerry, whose story we told at the close of the last chapter. His last meeting with his father was so traumatic and painful that he was almost frozen in a perpetual state of emotional anguish. He was afraid of being hurt again if he tried to re-establish contact with his father, but the pain deep inside from being separated hurt just as badly. Thankfully, Jerry discovered how to find value in troubled times, and he was able to begin the process of "unthawing" emotionally and moving away from his pain.

It is certainly not wrong to avoid pain when we can. But it is wrong to deny problems, ignore them, or try to explain them away.[2] One of the all-time-great truths is that life is difficult and often unfair. The better we are at seeing through trials to what they can produce in our lives and our children's lives, the better able we'll be to provide calmness, assurance, and genuine love to our children, even in the midst of trying times. In fact, trials have the capacity to bring strength, maturity, courage, genuine love, righteousness, and perseverance to those who are willing to be trained by them.[3] The very things we fear might happen to our children can make them stronger people, depending on their response and our response to their difficulties.

Before we proceed any further on this point, we want to set the record straight. We're not saying that parents should stand by and let children suffer trials if it's within their power to help them, nor that parents should create or actively seek out difficulties children can experience.

The apostle Paul was asked whether we should create evil that "grace may abound" (Romans 6:1). Put another way, should we cause troubled times for our children so that God can build good things into their lives? In Greek, his answer was *Me Genota*.[4] That's the strongest way possible in his language to say, "Absolutely not! No way! Don't even think about it!"

Children who are mistreated may one day gain positive things from the trials they experience, but that is because of God's grace, not their parents' sin. It would be better for a millstone to be hung around our necks than to deliberately hurt any little one.[5]

In this chapter, we'll take a closer look at what we mean by trials coming wrapped as opportunities for growth. We'll also suggest three actions you can take that set the stage for finding value in troubled times. Then in the next chapter, we'll describe five specific benefits that can be a part of any trial you or your children experience. While our emphasis will be on teaching children to uncover these benefits, those who grew up in difficult home situations can apply this as the basis of being free to give honor to their parents. These are the same steps that helped Jerry begin to honor his father.

WHEN HURT COMES WRAPPED UP AS OPPORTUNITY

Several years ago, we heard a story about a man who was walking along the sidewalk outside his high-rise apartment. It was early on a bitterly cold winter morning, and he was headed for the local twenty-four-hour convenience store. Suddenly, from out of nowhere it seemed, he was hit on the shoulder by a heavy object and knocked to the ground.

For several moments he lay on the sidewalk, trying to clear his head and feeling to see if his shoulder was broken. Finally, he sat up and looked around. The street was deserted, so he ruled out having been hit by a car. He looked up at the apartments above him, but he could see no open windows.

Struggling to his feet, he looked around one more time and saw a shoe box lying near him. It was heavily taped from end to end. As he bent down to pick it up, he found it was so heavy he had to use both hands.

Later that morning, as he sat in his apartment nursing his bruised, hurting shoulder, he took his scissors and cut through the tape wrapped around the box. Lifting the lid, he saw three fairly large cloth sacks in the box. As he lifted out one of the sacks and opened it in the light, he gasped and sat back in his chair. There were dozens of small gold bars and coins!

Talking to the police, he was told that more than likely, the gold had been stolen jewelry that had been melted down. Whether it had fallen from an apartment or from a plane overhead, they could never determine. However, after he waited six months to see if anyone claimed the gold, the shoe box legally became his property.

Most of us would suffer through a sore shoulder to end up with a box filled with gold! However, we have a similar opportunity to find value when we are hit by trials. Every trial is a box containing valuable treasures. It may knock us to the ground and bruise us, but once we learn how to open the box, we can find great gain inside.

For you who want God's very best,[6] He places in every trial you experience rare coins that are worth a great deal. This is true even if those trials include being hated by your brothers, nearly losing your life, being sold for pennies into a foreign slave market, being framed for adultery, being thrown into jail without a trial, and then being forgotten by the very person who could have won your release. At least that was Joseph's perspective after he experienced all the above![7] Looking back on all the trials he went through at the hands of his brothers, he was able to say to the very ones who caused him such problems, "But as for you, you meant evil against me; but God meant it for *good*, in order to bring it about as it is this day, to save many people alive."[8]

You have the privilege of explaining to your children that each trial contains value. Some have more value built into them than others; some of the less painful trials you experience may not be as valuable as the more painful ones you struggle through. Trials are painful, but unwrapping them to see what they can produce in your lives can be a tremendous source of help for you and your children.

How do you honor a child helping him find value through

trials? To answer this, let's start by looking at an example close to home. Over the years, I (Gary) have had to repeatedly unwrap trials with my younger son, Michael.

A CASE STUDY IN CATASTROPHES

For some reason, Michael is the accident-prone one in the family. When he was two weeks old, he almost died from severe stomach problems that required major surgery. For the next several years, he suffered through a series of childhood illnesses, but when he was three years old, he went through two terrible trials.

First, I was digging in the back yard and unearthed a yellow jacket nest. Sadly, Mike happened to be standing right where the nest came out, and he was stung repeatedly before I could get him inside. Then in the same year, Mike nearly drowned in a motel swimming pool. It was only by means of mouth-to-mouth resuscitation that we were able to revive him.

Since then, Mike has fallen off everything and onto anything possible in our house. And his accidents aren't limited to our home. We were at a business associate's home one evening when Mike was young, and they were rough-housing in the living room. Our friend was swinging Mike around by his feet just for fun when he suddenly lost his grip and Mike smashed into the coffee table, splitting his head open.

For as long as I can remember, Mike has had something in his mouth. At first it was a retainer to enlarge his mouth and then braces to pull his teeth in tighter. From accidents to inconveniences, you name it and Mike has experienced it. And it doesn't seem as though he's slowing down a bit as the years go by!

This past summer, at age thirteen, he was in a major car accident, and he broke his nose and his arm. He was showered with so much broken glass, it took the doctors two hours to take out all the glass slivers from the side of his face and from his eyelid (thankfully, it never penetrated to his eye).

What do you say to a child who has gone through so many trials? Let us tell you now the three actions we promised to describe earlier, the approach we take during and after each trial. These principles aren't in the form of a simple formula that you can wave over a hurting child and use to take away his pain. Rather, they are attitudes and actions you can develop toward suffering, actions that begin with your very first response.

BUILDING VALUE THROUGH TROUBLED TIMES

1. Helping Your Child Grow through Trials Begins with Your First Response.

Have you ever seen a toddler fall down and then turn around and look up before he decided whether or not to cry? Very often, a child's first response is to look to his parents when a trial comes to get some kind of reading on how worried he should be.

Often, the first response by parents can set the tone for how traumatically an event will be taken. When an accident occurs, a breakup with a boyfriend or girlfriend takes place, or there's a problem with someone at school, we've found that being soft and calmly accepting when our children first come to us does several positive things. For one thing, it gives them energy they need at the moment—energy to deal constructively with the problem. With my (Gary's) children, I've seen this time and again.

When Kari was eighteen years old, she slammed into the back of a car during a terrible rainstorm. The accident occurred when another woman tried to turn left from the wrong lane. That also turned out to be the day that Kari received a vivid lesson in differing responses to trials.

Norma and I were away when she got home, but one of our friends had dropped by the house to see us. When he saw the damaged car, he burst into angry words and lectured her about what a careless driver she was and how she could have killed herself or someone else. Just about that time, we pulled into the driveway. Kari was already crying over what this friend had said, and when we got out of the car, she cried even harder.

At that first moment, all we did was hold her and let her tell us the story. In a little while, she was able to wipe her eyes and smile for the first time. Our friend was so surprised by the contrast, he apologized to Kari for being so upset with her. He may have learned in his home that hurts were first met with angry words or emotions, not softness and a gentle touch.

When one of my children is hurting, compounding it by reacting with angry words doesn't add to the solution. If anything, such a reaction often freezes things in a problem state.

Responding with initial softness helps the child see that if Dad and Mom aren't panicking, maybe there is a light at the end of the tunnel. If the child sees his parents panicking or moving into anger, he is often barred from responding in any other way.

> When parents know ahead of time that the very things that have potential to devalue their children can be used by God to build character into their lives, they are strengthening their grip on their emotions.

One young boy we counseled with told us how difficult it was to share minor hurts or problems with his mother because every negative thing was blown way out of proportion. Once he came home from school and told her that he thought he may have flunked a test. Dropping the mixing bowl, she threw up her hands and began crying. "What are we going to do with you?" she said between sobs. "What are we going to do?"

How did such a response affect her son, who was the one experiencing the trial? "When my mom would panic like that, I can remember thinking, *How do I know what we're going to do with me? I'm only in the tenth grade! That's why I came to you!*"

Where does the ability to initiate softness and keep from panicking come from? *From a decision forged in quiet times apart from trials to believe that God works all things unto good* (Romans 8:28).[9]

In the middle of a fire, there isn't time to think about ways to prevent a fire. Parents who react emotionally in anger or panic to problems instead of having a plan for responding to them can increase the tension in the air. When parents know ahead of time that the very things that have the potential to devalue their children can be used by God to build character into their lives, they are strengthening their grip on their emotions.

When Michael was in his serious automobile accident this past summer, my first words to him could have been a lecture, something like these: "Were you wearing your seat belt, young man? What was the driver doing? Did you distract him?" or "Mike, did you know that this makes the ten thousandth time you've been banged up? *Did you?* Do you have any idea how embarrassing it is to send in another claim form on you? *Do you?* Do you realize that it's senseless accidents like yours that are causing health care costs in the country to rise dramatically?"

Even if I hadn't been angry and lectured him, I could have used my most pious voice at the hospital and said, "Michael, do you realize how exciting this is? You're going to grow so much spiritually from this! Don't you want to thank God right now that you're hurting so much?" When Mike lay in the hospital room, all Norma and I did was lovingly and calmly stand by him and encourage him through the initial pain.

The book of Proverbs says that having enthusiasm in the face of sorrow is like walking outside on a bitterly cold day without a coat (Proverb 25:20). Meeting someone else's trial with enthusiastic words about how much he can learn through the pain he's suffering can do much the same thing. When a difficulty first happens, don't lecture your children, panic, or become sickeningly pious. Calmly comforting them at the beginning of a trial lays the foundation for them to find value in their experience. Calmness comes from within us when we are confident in God's Word. Painful trials produce maturity, which leads to love! (See James 1:2 and Hebrews 12:10, 11.)

2. Keep Tabs on Your Child's Thinking Process During and Following the Trial.

People in California who have lived through several earthquakes know the truth of the old baseball slogan, It ain't over 'til it's over. The first quake may have ended, but they know better than to let their guard down or move back into their houses too soon. It's likely there will be aftershocks that can be nearly as deadly as the first quake.

A similar thing is true when you help your children deal with trials. You need to learn to listen and watch for their reactions following trials to make sure that the aftershocks of emotion won't chip away at their self-worth.

Are they disappointed? Are they angry? Those emotions are common and normal. But are they *staying* angry? Are they repeatedly discouraged? Do they get depressed easily after the event? Does everything have a way of directing their attention back to that trying time, or do they try just as hard to avoid mentioning the subject?

After your children have experienced a trial, you should stand back and watch what's happening with them. If they continue to struggle, you can move in to help them. If they are handling the problem well, you can be just as quick to encourage their response to the trial.

We've observed that when people go through a painful experience, it often enables them to go through a similar experience in the future with less effect. Michael had already been through so many things that the automobile accident wasn't that traumatic for him. Even during the two hours they worked to take all the glass from his face, he was calm and joked with his brother who was "helping" in surgery. A week after the accident, Mike's attitude was still positive when he learned that he'd have to go through the Arizona summer with a cast on his arm and wouldn't be able to swim.

Watching Mike's attitude gave us an opportunity to praise

him for the way he was handling the situation. However, several months after the accident, we make a mental note to keep tabs on what's happening with his response to that trial. By doing so, we can spot early warning signs like depression or anxiety that could grow into major problems later on.

3. A Few Days After a Trial, Look for an Opportunity to Discuss How God Could Use It in Your Child's Life.

When is the best time to say that there is value in troubled times? How can you do it in a way that sounds genuine, not saccharine sweet? Perhaps several days or weeks may go by before a child is ready to hear the message that God can bring forth value in troubled times.

One way I bring up the subject is to say, "Are you satisfied with what you're experiencing out of the trial you've been through?"

If he hasn't talked about the trial yet, almost always he'll say, "No, I'm not. I'm miserable and unhappy."

At this point I may ask, "Would you like to spend some time this week 'unwrapping' the trial you've received?" I may also give him a hug and a reassuring smile or look.

If his answer is yes (and nine times out of ten it is), that's when I can discuss with him what God's Word has to say about troubled times—the very things we'll be saying in the next chapter. If his answer is no, I don't panic. I just come back another day and softly but persistently give him the opportunity to open up the box his trial came in to see the precious coins inside.

When you teach your children what God's Word has to say about troubled times, you're providing a lamp unto their feet.[10] Biblical principles are like powerful flashlights that can light up even the darkest trial your children may experience.

Because you know this, you can verbally and nonverbally convey this message to your children as they watch your response to their trials. And you can also ask them if they are willing to look for what God has to teach them in the difficulty they've experienced.

One man's life provides a dramatic answer to the question, Can God indeed bring positives out of troubled times?

This young man's name is David, and he is an awesome picture of God's using difficulties for good.[11] For years he viewed trials as something that affected only his external world, and any blow to what he owned or how he looked would discourage him and leave him feeling cheated.

Today, David travels around the world, talking with people about how he discovered that no matter what happens to the outside, it's the internal life that trials really touch. Just like what happened in Jerry's life (whose story we shared in the last chapter), the bigger the trial, the more potential to see God's power and peace at work in the inner person.

FINDING VALUE IN THE WORST OF TRIALS

During the Vietnam War, David went through rigorous training to become part of the ultraelite special forces team the navy used on dangerous search-and-destroy missions. During a nighttime raid on an enemy stronghold, David experienced the greatest trial of his life. When he and his men were pinned down by enemy machine-gun fire, he pulled a phosphorus grenade from his belt and stood up to throw it. But as he pulled back his arm, a bullet hit the grenade, and it exploded next to his ear.

Lying on his side on the bank of a muddy river, he watched part of his face float by. His entire face and shoulder alternately smoldered and caught on fire as the phosphorus that had embedded itself in his body came into contact with the air.

David knew that he was going to die, yet miraculously he didn't. He was pulled from the water by his fellow soldiers, flown directly to Saigon, and then taken to a waiting plane bound for Hawaii. But David's problems were just beginning.

When he first went into surgery—the first of what would become dozens of operations—the surgical team had a major problem during the operation. As they cut away tissue that had been burned or torn by the grenade, the phosphorus would hit the oxygen in the operating room and begin to ignite again! Several times the doctors and nurses ran out of the room, leaving him alone because they were afraid the oxygen used in surgery would explode! Incredibly, David survived the operation and was taken to a ward that held the most severe burn and injury cases from the war.

Lying on his bed, his head the size of a basketball, David knew he presented a grotesque picture. Although he had once been a handsome man, he knew he had nothing to offer his wife or anyone else because of his appearance. He felt more alone and more worthless than he had ever felt in his life.

But David wasn't alone in his room. There was another man who had been wounded in Vietnam and was also a nightmarish sight. He had lost an arm and a leg, and his face was badly torn and scarred.

As David was recovering from surgery, this man's wife arrived from the States. When she walked into the room and took one look at her husband, she became nauseated. She took off her wedding ring, put it on the nightstand next to him, and said, "I'm so sorry, but there's no way I could live with you looking like that." And with that, she walked out the door.

He could barely make any sounds through his torn throat and mouth, but the soldier wept and shook for hours. Two days later, he died.

That woman's attitude represents in many respects the way the world views a victim of accident or injury. If a trial emotionally or physically scars someone or causes him to lose his attractiveness, the world says "Ugly is bad," and consequently, any value that person feels he has to others is drained away.

For this poor wounded soldier, knowing that his wife saw no value in him was more terrible than the wounds he suffered. It blew away his last hope that someone, somewhere, could find worth in him because he knew how the world would perceive him.

Three days later, David's wife arrived. After watching what had happened with the other soldier, he had no idea what kind of reaction she would have toward him, and he dreaded her coming. His wife, a strong Christian, took one look at him, came over, and kissed him on the only place on his face that wasn't bandaged. In a gentle voice she said, "Honey, I love you. I'll always love you. And I want you to know that whatever it takes, whatever the odds, we can make it together." She hugged him where she could to avoid disturbing his injuries and stayed with him for the next several days.

Watching what had happened with the other man's wife and seeing his own wife's love for him gave David tremendous strength. More than that, her understanding and accepting him greatly reinforced his own relationship with the Lord.

In the weeks and months that followed, David's wounds slowly but steadily healed. It took dozens of operations and months of agonizing recovery, but today, miraculously, David can see and hear.

On national television, we heard David make an incredible statement.

I am twice the person I was before I went to Vietnam. For one thing, God has used my suffering to help me feel other people's pain and to have an incredible burden to reach people for Him. The Lord has let me have a worldwide, positive effect on people's lives because of what I went through.

I wouldn't trade anything I've gone through for the benefits my trials have had in my life, on my family's life and on countless teenagers and adults I've had the opportunity to influence over the years.[12]

David experienced a trial that no parents would wish on their children. Yet in spite of all the tragedy that surrounded him, God turned his troubled times into fruitful ones.

Knowing that the almighty Creator of the universe can take the greatest trials and use them to His glory should be an encouragement to us as parents. The same God who can trade tears of agony for the oak of righteousness (Isaiah

61:3) can take our children's trials and build value into their lives.

In the next chapter, we'll look specifically at five assets that lay wrapped up in each trial our children or we ourselves can open and experience. These are positive elements that can build self-worth and high value into our lives.

CHAPTER FIVE

Helping Our Children Find Value in Troubled Times: Part 2

Seeing my (Gary's) son lying on a blood-stained stretcher, not moving, with a plastic brace taped to his head, I thought that he wouldn't live through this one. The paramedics calmed me down by assuring me he had only minor injuries and would recover rapidly.

Some of my earliest thoughts were, *What possible benefit did that have? What benefit is there in any trial a child may go through?* I was already assured by the Scriptures and my own experiences that God could and would use this trial in our lives for great benefit to us and glory to Himself. Today, I'm aware of at least five positive benefits that came out of that trial and that we've seen to be wrapped up in any trial. These are benefits that parents can point out to their children and thus raise their value through troubled times.

That's not to say that people can't become bitter or deeply angry when they experience a traumatic experience or loss. Nor does it explain away healthy tears that should be cried nor condone negative actions of others that may have caused the pain. But when we learn to teach our children that God can bring good out of trials, we take the first step in opening up their lives to these positive effects.

WHEN OUR CHILDREN EXPERIENCE
TROUBLED TIMES . . .

1. They Can Gain an Increased Awareness of Others' Needs and Pain.

In Shakespeare's *Romeo and Juliet,* Romeo says, "He jests at scars, that never felt a wound."[1] For many people who have never been through any kind of deep emotional pain, empathy can remain only a dictionary definition.

Dr. Gary Collins, a Christian psychologist, says that the mark of a person who truly knows how to **love** others and be an effective "people helper" is being able to empathize with their pain.[2] Children or adults who go through difficult times almost always gain a deeper understanding and compassion toward others' needs and pain. For example, we know of a pastor in the Midwest whose counseling ministry was transformed by a major trial he faced.

Bob is a tremendous teacher, but by his own admission he has always struggled in the area of counseling. He wasn't a good listener to people who were hurting, and he tended to cover even the most difficult problem with a hastily found verse and a quick closing prayer.

Although he wouldn't say it to anyone who came into his office, deep inside he often felt that people who came in "crying" were just weak and weren't trusting God with their problems. They simply needed to tighten their belts and "gut it up." But that all changed one afternoon when news arrived of his father's sudden death.

Bob and his father had the natural ties of a father and son, but they were best friends, too. And while he knew his mother had health problems, his father's sudden death due to an aneurysm took him totally by surprise.

Bob had preached at dozens of funerals, but suddenly *he* was the one sitting in the front row with the family. For the first time in his life, his heart went through the anguish of losing a loved one, and it changed him forever—by softening and sensitizing his heart.

Today, Bob is still a tremendous pastor and teacher, but he has more depth to his messages. And since his father's death, he has listened more and cried more with the people in his congregation than in all the other years of his ministry combined.

Bob became aware of what we feel made King David able to write such moving, emotional psalms. In many ways, they both knew the heartbreaking pain of suffering.

The psalmist who wrote the uplifting words, "O Lord, our Lord, / How excellent is Your name in all the earth" (Psalm 8:1), was the same who wrote, "All night I make my bed swim; / I drench my couch with my tears. / My eye wastes away because of grief" (Psalm 6:6–7).

In spite of all his glorious victories, cheering crowds, and magnificent prayers, there were many times when David cried himself to sleep. He was hunted down in the desert by a man who had once loved him.[3] He grieved over the death of his best friend, Jonathan.[4] His wife grew to despise him and his devotion to God and mocked him to his face.[5] He had a rebellious son whose attempt to overthrow David's throne ended in the young man's brutal death.[6] David's own sin left one man dead and a woman in shame and eventually led to the death of a little baby he helped conceive out of wedlock.[7]

David was able to write about a Shepherd who walked with him through the valley of the shadow of death because he had been there. Hunted down by those who had once said they loved him, he slipped into the inky blackness of trials, yet he came out into God's light. The same thing can remain true for any of us today.

Like David, Nancy went through a terrible ordeal of physical and emotional pain, but her suffering was caused by her father's sexual abuse. For three years, she experienced perhaps the greatest blow imaginable to a person's sense of value and self-worth from a man who should have been her greatest encourager and help.

When parents violate a child's boundaries in this way, they cut as deeply as the greatest hurt and can leave lasting scars that can affect a young boy or girl for life.[8] But in Nancy's case, those scars have also brought an incredible sensitivity. Although we can't explain exactly how, Nancy can spend only a few moments with other women, and she can sense with uncanny accuracy those who have been abused sexually.

There was nothing good in what Nancy suffered in her dishonoring home. Yet good has come out of it. Without any formal training, she has a tremendously effective "coffee cup counseling" ministry with other women suffering the effects of abuse.

In my (Gary's) home, there is no question about who is the most sensitive person. No one feels the hurt of others or even of animals as deeply as Mike does, and he is the one who has suffered the most. By pointing this out to Mike and by sharing with him how much God will be able to use that sensitivity in his own family and ministry in the years to come, I've seen his eyes brighten as he sees positive gain in his trials.

How often in our own lives has someone ministered to us during a difficult time with caring eyes and loving concern, and later we learned that person had been through a similar trial? The writer of the book of Hebrews tells us that Jesus is able to aid those who suffer because of what He Himself suffered (Hebrews 2:18).

As you begin to look for and teach your children about positive gains through trials, one clear benefit is that God can make them more aware of others' hurts. This increased sensitivity can help them become individuals who help others, and it is a **major factor** in their ability to genuinely love others.

2. They Can Learn Humility.

One common denominator in facing difficult times is that they are almost always humbling. Whether it's the boy who fell while walking up the steps at school or the girl who had such a hard time explaining her divorce at the ten-year reunion, trying experiences often bring people back to rock bottom.

After Mike's automobile accident, several scars remain on his cheek, his eyelid, and his lip. Since he is in junior high, walking around with scars on his face can be humbling. Of course, at first it was something to brag about with the guys; but as time has passed, even though the doctor has assured us the scars will eventually become less noticeable, it's been a very humbling experience for Mike.

What possible benefit is there in being humbled? Do these verses sound familiar? "Blessed are the meek,/For they shall inherit the earth" (Matthew 5:5). "God resists the proud,/But gives grace to the humble" (James 4:6). One lifelong benefit you receive from going through painful situations is the increase of God's grace. You get more of His undeserved, unearned favor[9] and more of His power to live successfully.

Recently, we were on a friend's radio call-in program. During the breaks when we were off the air, we learned about this man's childhood. As a boy, he had been assaulted sexually by a relative. The experience was so traumatic for him that he was never able to tell his parents, who loved him dearly and treated him accordingly. In a sense, he has felt that the relative robbed him of the blessing his parents gave him.

Because he was so ashamed of what had happened to him, the tragedy of that event would rush to his mind every time he accomplished something significant and keep him from enjoying it. Even though he had reached the top of his profession, he had terrible insecurities and doubts about himself. But in the last year, he had learned an important truth.

In studying the Scriptures, he ran across a statement the Lord directed to Paul: "My grace is sufficient for you" (2 Corinthians 12:9). Paul was experiencing a trial that was humbling to him, and he wished God would take it from his life. Yet he lived out his life with his thorn in the flesh and the words, "My grace is sufficient for you."

As our friend thought about his own trial that had humbled him so much, he suddenly remembered another verse, "God gives grace to the humble." He had certainly been humbled, and he knew God's grace was sufficient. But at last he put the two together, and the words moved from his head to his heart.

Our friend is one of the best counselors we know, with a tremendous sensitivity to hurting people who call in. Every time we're with him, we listen in wonder at how accurately he can pinpoint what a caller is struggling with, even though he has learned only a few details of the situation. Yet he admits that he would never have been as effective in feeling compassion and helping others in pain had he not gone through what he did.

While the experience itself was and continues to be a heinous sin and a humbling incident, God's grace has proved more than sufficient. That relative left our friend's self-worth in "ashes," but God has turned the negative effects of the experience into beauty in his life.

Being Humbled Can Teach Us Lessons in Helping Others. Being humbled by a trial showers us with God's grace and also helps us become better servants. That may not sound too appealing to some people who have no desire to be servants. After all, servants have a low social status, don't they? When God counts valuable people, however, they're the first He points to, and He says they're the greatest (Matthew 20:26). Do you know what Jesus said was the highest calling in life? Not preaching. Not teaching. Not even evangelism. But *serving* (John 13:1ff.).

I (John) found that being humbled made me a better servant. When I was entering high school, my mother had to go through a series of operations due to her rheumatoid arthritis. We used to call her the "Bionic Woman" because she had so many artificially replaced joints that she had to carry a card to get through the metal detector at airports.

During much of her recuperative time, my mother had to walk very slowly using a cane or use a wheelchair that one of us boys would push. Pushing a woman around in a wheelchair might have gotten me a merit badge if I had been a Boy Scout, but in the crowd I hung around with before I became a Christian, it only brought mocking and abuse.

To be very honest, it was humbling at times. But do you know what I quickly learned? The humiliation I felt at the hands of a few callous friends made me a better servant. Even though I was in high school, responding to my mother's needs taught me incredible lessons in servanthood.

Those lessons I learned in my teens are still helping me today in my ministry with others and with my own family.

Being humbled helps us gain more of God's grace, and the power of His grace in us provides the ability to enrich the lives of others. That ability, in turn, increases our sense of self-worth. In Lori's case, it did more than that. It held the key to how God would use her in the future.

For years, Lori hated herself and even God for making her the way she was. Many little girls were taller than the boys in grade school, but as time passed, Lori kept her height advantage. Feeling self-conscious and alone, she adopted eating habits that soon left her with a weight problem, too.

She just knew that being born big boned and heavyset had reduced her chances of getting dates, and she hated the way she stood out in a crowd. Even after she became a Christian during high school, she couldn't find a single thing to thank God for when it came to her appearance.

Then one day Lori's high-school business education class visited a nearby hospital on a career field trip. That afternoon Lori's life changed on the spot, and it happened when they were visiting the physical therapy room.

As the class stood listening to a nurse tell about the different equipment being used in the room, a minor emergency occurred. A young woman with a spinal cord injury slid from her exercise machine onto the floor. As the girl began to cry, almost without thinking Lori hurried to lift her up and put her gently in her wheelchair. It would have been a task for at least two nurses, but Lori's size enabled her to lift the girl with ease.

It has been seven years since that field trip, and when we talked to Lori last year, here's what she said about it: "For years I looked at the way God made me as a curse, not a blessing. But that day at the hospital, I learned that He could use me just the way He made me! That young woman needed my strong arms. That afternoon, for the first time in my life I was able to thank God for who I was and even for making me big."

Lori has completed occupational therapy training, and today she is on the staff of a major southwestern hospital, feeling valued and needed as she serves hurting children and adults—just the way God made her.

Trials can be humbling. It may not be pleasant if your child drops a pass in the end zone, is the only one to forget a piece at the piano recital, wets the bed at a friend's slumber party, or has to repeat the second grade; but your child can receive God's grace when it happens. Trials can make his heart more sensitive to others, and God may use them to make him a better servant in years to come. For some children, trials can hold the key to discovering life-time goals.

3. The Trials Can Deepen Their Maturity and Give Them Endurance.

Have you ever noticed that many people who suffer tend to develop a maturity and strength far beyond their years? Carol benefited from her trials in that very way. She lived in a single-parent home with her mother who was an alcoholic. In high school, she was definitely part of the "in" crowd, but in some ways she stood apart from them. Because of the things she suffered at home, Carol made some decisions early in life that many of her more immature friends had to learn the hard way.

When the group began to take bottles to parties, Carol had already seen where social drinking could lead. Her girlfriends had never seen someone passed out on the floor, lying in her own vomit. Carol had. And the pictures of her mother made it easier for her to say no to the offers to "share a drink." Seeing the part alcohol played in her parents' divorce also made her set her dating standards higher than those of many of her friends.

People who come from alcoholic homes are more likely to become alcoholics than those who come from nonalcoholic homes. Often a person coming from an alcoholic home has such a low self-value that she acts out her low worth by repeating her parents' problems. However, instead of being controlled by the trials she experienced, Carol learned how to look for positive things in her background that could build her worth.

For Carol, coming from an alcoholic home acted as a deterrent to drinking. In addition, she was working and maintaining an after-school job and a household long before many of her friends. She learned lessons in responsibility then that helped her in her career and with her own husband and children.

Growing up too soon can be a hurtful trial. Yet today, years after she has left home, Carol is able to thank God for the responsibility and maturity her trials built into her life. In her endurance and capacity to deal with difficulties, she's head and shoulders above many her age. And there are others like her—Alan, for instance.

Alan's sister died of leukemia when she was a senior in high school and he was a freshman. As devastating as that trial was, he changed greatly after her death. Suddenly, little things he had once taken for granted took on a more precious nature. Alan ceased to look at life and death and spiritual things in a childish way. The growth and maturity that event wrought in his life helped carve out a capacity to care and a burden to share Christ with others that have made him one of the finest pastors in the country today.

As in Carol's and Alan's lives, nature has its own way of picturing this spiritual truth. Every fall, those of us with yards have to go through the ritual of "scalping" our grass. Cutting it down so short makes it seem it will be forever kept from sprouting. Yet every spring, it grows up even more lush and green because of the cutting. The Scriptures tell us that every branch that bears fruit, the Lord prunes back at times to help it grow and bear more fruit (John 15:1–8). As difficult as the pruning process is, the results are the fruit of the Spirit that can change our lives and those around us (Galatians 5:22).

No one who is familiar with Joni Eareckson Tada's story will deny the beautiful life God made from her terrible accident. When she is on a television program or a radio talk show, her maturity radiates how much God has taught her through her suffering. Maturity is a third wonderful benefit you can look for and point out as you honor your children by helping them find value in troubled times.

In a healthy body, when one member of the body suffers,

all the other parts suffer along with it (1 Corinthians 12:26). The same thing is true in a healthy family. When one person suffers, the rest of the family can be drawn closer through the sharing of that sorrow. That's the fourth benefit of going through trials.

4. The Difficult Times Can Draw Us Together as a Family.

One of the most emotional experiences we've witnessed was the closing moments of a reunion of World War II veterans. A few summers ago we were staying at a hotel in The Loop in Chicago where a reunion of former tank artillerymen and commanders for General Patton was being held. The officers and men had fought from Italy to France and made a heroic rescue of surrounded Allied troops at the Battle of the Bulge. Most of them had lost a number of close friends in the war. All of them had experienced major trials together.

We were in the lobby when the reunion was breaking up and many of the men were saying their good-byes. In one way, it was almost comical. Because of the incredible noise inside the tanks when their cannon were fired (tankmen in World War II didn't have the protective equipment artillerymen do today), many of the men suffered severe hearing loss.

As a result parting conversations were much louder than they would be for people with normal hearing, and requests to get the other person to repeat something he had just said were commonplace. Yet in spite of all that, we will never forget the tears, the embraces, and the love the men showed for one another over forty years after they had fought together. They may have lost their ability to hear as they once could, but their ability to love one another more than made up for it.

Experiencing troubled times welded these men together into a family. When children experience a trial, it can have a similar effect on each member of the family.

For years, when I (Gary) asked my son Michael, "Why

does Dad love you so much?" he would smile and say, "Because I brought you back to the family."

Michael came along at a time when I was at the "height" of my career. The other children were getting older, and I was able to travel more to minister to others. At the time, the last thing I wanted was more responsibility around the house.

To be honest, in some ways I resented Michael in those first days when we brought him home from the hospital. But all that changed one day when we were swimming in a motel pool and I looked over to see three-year-old Michael's small body at the bottom.

I'll never forget thinking, *Oh, Lord, we've lost him,* as I dived into the deep end and brought him up to the surface. Laying him on the side of the pool, I gave him mouth-to-mouth resuscitation, and very shortly he coughed and began to cry. From that moment on, it was as if that trial bonded me to Michael in a special way and brought me back to the family. That experience was a major reason for my asking my boss for a different job that would keep me off the road and closer to home.

Throughout the years, trials that the other children have experienced have drawn the rest of us closer together as well. But because of all that has happened to Michael, it seems God has used him time and again to pull us together as a family. Take last Christmas, for instance.

A favorite tradition around the Smalley household is having a marinated steak fondue on Christmas Day. We were all busy sticking pieces of bread and steak with the long fondue forks and dipping them into the fondue when Michael suddenly let out a blood-curdling scream!

As he tried to stick his fork through a piece of steak, it slipped and rammed all the way through the palm of his hand! For several minutes while Greg and I ran for pliers to cut the fork loose and Norma and Kari ministered to Michael, pandemonium broke loose in our house.

Finally, after we had bandaged his hand and he was feeling much better, Michael began to laugh. Soon we were all rolling on the floor laughing at the hectic things that had happened with all of us running around and shouting.

When everyone quieted down, Michael looked at me with a smile and said, *"Hey, why is it that I'm always the one who brings the family back together?"*

Have you been able to identify a common thread that runs through the benefits we've discussed so far? They can all help children become more loving.

5. They Can Become More Loving.

The greatest coin we can discover as we unwrap any trial is love. Troubled times have a way of cutting deep channels into our lives that can carry God's love to us and our love to others.

In the weeks after my son's car accident, I had the opportunity to sit down with him several times and list some of the benefits that were a part of his trial. Because we've done this with so many of his trials, he was quick to point out ways in which he had become more sensitive, had gained maturity, and had seen the positive side of his humbling scars. Yet the greatest gift trials can bring him is their ability to make him more loving.

Perhaps the thing I appreciate the most about people like Joni and my son, Michael, is the deep love for the Lord and for others that has developed through trials. As C. S. Lewis said, "God speaks to us in our joys; He shouts to us in our sorrows."[10] People who look for and thank God in advance for the benefits He can bring through a trial not only help themselves, but they can also look for and share these principles with their children.

Children don't have to be shut up in their pain forever. Our God is as good as His Word, and His Word tells us that all things work together for good for those who love Him (Romans 8:28). He is so trustworthy, we can thank Him before seeing immediate benefits from our trials (1 Thessalonians 5:18). In the process of time and with loving parents to help them cut the tape and remove the lid from difficult times, sons and daughters can gain love through the trials that once threatened to take it from them.

FURTHER HELP ON FINDING BENEFITS
IN TRIALS

Before we close this chapter, we have a few other comments to make about how to respond to trials. With problems such as unwanted pregnancy, major accidents, cancer, death of a parent, and other traumatic events, don't expect your child to see benefits from his trial overnight. In some cases, it may take a year or longer.

For Nancy, whose story of abuse we shared earlier, it took almost a year of continually looking for positive benefits from her abusive background before she was able to see anything positive from that terrible experience. However, once she began to see how God had made her more sensitive, a better servant, and more loving to her own family and others, she was able to make a decision to forgive her father and for the first time move away from the pain of the past. Every day for almost eight months Jerry, who struggled with his father, had to make a decision to unwrap his trials and look for benefits God had supplied him before he too loosened the painful grip of the past.

Experts say that it takes at least thirty days of repeating something consistently before it becomes ingrained as a habit. You need to be lovingly persistent in looking for positive benefits God has worked or will provide in your life if you're to find value in troubled times.

We're not explaining away the possibility that some people can go through difficulties and become anything but more loving in the process. It's natural for someone to go through a stage where he's angry over what has happened to him, but making a decision to *remain* angry can desensitize him to spiritual truth. That decision can lead to bitterness and resentment. It can harden his heart and weaken his relationship with God and others.

The mark of a person who does or does not grow through trials is not the amount of tears he has cried. It is the degree to which he is willing to take God at His word. If he only listens to the wisdom of the world, trials that touch him on the outside will almost always lower his sense of value. If he listens to God's unchanging Word, however, even when it is only a still, small voice amidst the storm or a troubled time, his inner life can be opened to maturity and gain.

Why sit down with your children and teach them that there can be value in trying times? Because of something Solomon, the wisest man who ever lived, once said:

> Remember now your Creator
>   in the days of your youth,
> Before the difficult days come,
> And the years draw near when you say,
> "I have no pleasure in them."
> (Ecclesiastes 12:1)

If you consistently ignore the benefits that can come from trials, you can watch the joy go out of your life. As Solomon said, if you live long enough, you will see enough sorrow and storm clouds to make your joy of living disappear.

If you're wise, you'll turn your children toward what God can build in their lives, even during trials, *before* the harsh realities of life rob them of their joy. This process begins by reminding them and yourself that where there is defeat, that's where God's strength is available. Where there is loneliness, that's where God's presence is. Wherever there are bad things happening to you, there is God giving you the power to gain value in Him and to serve and love others in need.

Let's now turn our gaze on another aspect of honor, recognizing our own parenting strengths and style.

CHAPTER SIX

Recognizing Our Own Parenting Strengths and Style

Twice, in quick succession, her father slaps her across the mouth as he firmly takes hold of her arm. "You little smart mouth!" he shouts at his ten-year-old daughter. "Keep it up! I've got all day to see to it that you clean up your room!"

Mother is now in the battle trying to defend Geri, her youngest daughter, but it's much too late. Dad has already lost control of his temper and stands screaming at her, "I want this room to look perfect! Look at these socks behind the door. Does this room look clean to you? You can forget about going over to your friend's house this afternoon. Starting now, you're grounded for a month. Do you hear me, young lady?" he yells into her ear as if she were deaf.

Why are some children raised with so much severity while others live in a healthier, more relaxed home? Why do some parents have incredible expectations of their children, but others encourage and motivate them to reach their own potential? Why do some homes seem to produce confident children, but others send sons or daughters away feeling insecure and unstable?

What we continue to see in our work with families is that parents who understand and develop their own particular positive parenting style raise confident children who feel of high worth. In other words, parents who have a better understanding of *who they are* and *what their strengths are* honor their children and build value into their lives.

In this chapter, we'll be discussing the four most common types of parents we see and the strengths they bring to the parenting task. Although there are numerous excellent individual personality books and tests on the market, we want to look at how these different individual "bents" can build value into children.

Also, we've found that while a person may act one way at work or with friends, he often has a different bent when it comes to his parenting style and how he relates to his children. Why is it so important for parents to understand their strengths in the parenting setting? I (John) discovered one vital reason on my first day of seminary.

UNDERSTANDING OUR PARENTING STRENGTHS

At the seminary I attended, all incoming students took the class "Bible Study Methods" that was taught by Dr. Howard Hendricks, a nationally known Christian educator and family expert. He was the finest equipper and discipler I've ever met, and his motivating courses on the Christian family were the very reasons why I decided to minister in the areas of counseling and family enrichment. To all of us at seminary, he was known affectionately as "Prof."

As I took my seat in the crowded classroom the first day, my anxiety was already sky high. Looking around the room, I knew that many of the men and women there had graduated from Christian colleges. Some had probably been to Christian grade schools and high schools as well.

Having graduated from a secular university and become a Christian just recently, I knew that I didn't have the background in Bible courses these students did. Would I pass the course? Could I make it through the rigors of the next four years? Was I smart enough to do the work?

After opening the class in prayer, the next thing Dr. Hendricks did raised my anxiety level another ten notches. In his brisk, energetic way, Prof pointed his finger at us and said, "Men and women, I'm about to give you a test. If you pass this test, I can almost guarantee you'll be successful in the ministry. If you fail this test, there's a great chance you'll wash out and won't make it. Now, get out a three-by-five card, and let me give you the test."

Oh no! I thought to myself as I fumbled for an index card. *He's going to ask us to name all the books in the Old Testament or list all the names in Christ's genealogy or at least give the "hidden" Greek meaning to some theological word that everybody who has been to Bible college already knows.*

With my head down, I was already thinking about what I would say to my family and friends when I flunked out of seminary. It was my first day in graduate school, and I already felt I was going to let down the Lord and my family.

Prof's words cut short my thoughts when he said, "On one side of the card, I'd like you to write down your three greatest weaknesses."

Three greatest weaknesses? That wasn't hard! The only difficult thing about that was limiting it to three. As I glanced around the room, I noticed that no one else seemed to have any trouble writing down weaknesses either. Pens moved furiously the next few minutes.

After a short time, Prof said, "Okay, that was the warm-up. Here's the real test."

I knew it! I said to myself. *Here comes the question about all the books in the Old Testament.*

Very deliberately, Prof said to us, "I want you to turn your index card over, and I want you to list your three greatest strengths."

It was so easy to write about weaknesses, but take time to write down strengths? After all, this was a Christian school, wasn't it? Shouldn't we talk only about our weaknesses? Even coming from a secular school, I knew that "pride cometh before a fall." Instead of the fast and furious writing of just a few moments ago, pens and pencils dangled in our hands as most of us struggled with our answers.

In the years that have passed since that "exam," I've often thought back to Prof's words when our time of writing was up. I can still picture him confidently stating, "In all my years of teaching, I've rarely met someone who can't quickly tell me his weaknesses. But if you don't know the strengths God has given you that you can develop, you'll never be a success in the ministry."

When we think about Christ's ministry, that statement makes very good sense. Our Lord knew who He was and where He had come from (John 16:5). He knew His relationship with His Father and what He could or would not do (John 5:19ff.). His confidence in the Scriptures made Him unafraid to meet even the most learned Pharisee in a face off of words.[1] In short, He knew His strengths and used them to serve God and us.

But how does this relate to you as a parent who wants to raise the value of your children? A parent who is aware of personal strengths is better able to serve children. If you can't write down three strengths you have right now, very likely your own value is so low you'll struggle in raising your children's worth above your own. Until you're aware of the strengths, characteristics, and traits God has built into your life, you can never understand your greatest weaknesses as a parent.

WHEN STRENGTHS BECOME PUSHED TO AN EXTREME

For most of us, our weaknesses are usually our strengths pushed to an extreme. That's worth repeating. Weaknesses are often strengths pushed to an extreme. Take the apostle Peter, for example.

When we think of Peter, the Rock, one strength he certainly had was his willingness to jump in wherever he sensed a need. On the day of Pentecost, this strength led him to preach such a powerful sermon that over three thousand people were saved. But what happened when that strength of "jumping in" was pushed to an extreme?

How about questioning whether Christ should go to the cross? Or nearly causing a massacre in the Garden of

Gethsemane when Jesus was being arrested, or quickly turning away from the Lord when several women questioned him before the Crucifixion?[2] Peter certainly had a strength in being quick to make up his mind. However, he often jumped regardless of the wisdom of doing so.

Maybe one of your strengths is making quick decisions. Being decisive can be a strength, but pushed to an extreme, it can lead you to become bossy or demanding.

Perhaps one of your strengths is listening. Taking the time to actively listen to a child can be a tremendous tool to build value into her life. But what happens when a person pushes the strength of listening to an extreme? Then you have a situation like Faye's.

Faye tried repeatedly to go to her mother for help with her problems. Every time Faye went to her mother with a major issue to discuss, however, she would listen, listen, listen. But because she felt insecure inside, she never felt confident enough to offer any suggestions to her daughter. Faye would often become so frustrated that she would say, "Mom, just tell me *something* I could do, would you?" Listening is a strength all of us need to develop, but for Faye's mother, it caused frustration instead of building value into her daughter.

Once a person understands what his strengths are, he becomes better able to recognize his weaknesses. An extremely conscientious mom can thank God for her natural bent toward orderliness, but she needs to guard against becoming obsessive with her house cleaning or excessively picky with the children. A dominant dad can thank God for his determination and efficiency, but he needs to guard against going too far with his dominance in the home and becoming harsh, pushy, and domineering.

There's one other reason why knowing your parenting style and strengths can help you. It helps you know which child you'll probably struggle with the most (the one with most of your same strengths), and how you can best encourage and equip each of your children by using their natural personality tendencies.

We know that there are parents reading this book who think they might not be able to come up with a single strength to put down on an index card. As you read about the four basic parenting styles, however, we hope you won't just look for areas you need to change. We hope that perhaps for the first time, you'll be able to see and thank God for your natural strengths, strengths you can use to build value in your children.

Are You a Take-Charge Charlene (or Charlie)?

Take-Charge (TC) parents like to get immediate results when they ask their children to do something. If they're really strong in this respect, their favorite line might be something like this, "When I tell you to jump, don't ask me why. Ask me how high."

They like challenges in life and may stir up a little excitement if things get too steady and relaxed. TC parents want to see results from the things to which they give their time (and money). They expect to see quick results like positive grades from their son who is being tutored or a minirecital from their daughter who is taking piano lessons.

TC parents speak directly and boldly. One great thing about TC parents is that you know just where you stand with them. Children don't need to guess whether Mom or Dad is angry, happy, or sad. It's right out in the open instead of being hidden behind a mask. However, as good as TC parents are in being forthright, they sometimes can say something very blunt to their children and walk away without realizing the possibly damaging impact of their words.

If TC parents have a teen-ager in the house, sparks can fly. TC parents don't like it when their children question the status quo, and they can get angry when they're questioned.

When talking to TC parents, children might find some resistance if they don't "get to the point" in sharing a request or story. TC parents aren't great chitchatters; they like to get on with conversations and get back to the challenges of life.

Finally, if TC parents see something they feel they need to respond to, they'll move right out. If they feel Bobby's room needs redecorating, they can spend hours that same afternoon shopping for new things. If Jayne wants to be the only child in her school who takes bagpipe lessons, within hours a TC parent can track down the only bagpipe tutor in town and get her child enrolled.

Like the apostle Peter, a TC person has the natural strength of decisive action, but she also needs to be sure she has talked to Bobby first about the decorating plan instead of changing his room when he's at school and figuring he'll appreciate all her efforts.

How can TC parents use their natural bent to build value into their children?

• By using their tendency to respond quickly to meet their children's or their spouse's needs.

• By speaking directly and without manipulation.

• By taking the lead to serve the family and setting a positive direction for family members to follow.

How can TC parents work to keep their strengths from being pushed into weaknesses?

• They can work on developing their sensitivity to other family members' feelings.

• They can slow down enough to let others ask questions and verbalize "why" they've made a decision. (We know of one TC father who never told his wife or children they were moving until he had already bought a house in a new city and put the For Sale sign up at their house!)

• They can pace themselves and make sure there are family fun times when everybody (including the TC parent) can relax.

Are You a Fun-Loving Freda (or Fred)?

If *Fun-Loving (FL) parents* were animals, without a doubt they'd be otters! Have you ever seen an otter in the wild or on film when he *didn't* look like he was having the time of his life? Even the act of opening an oyster or sliding down a hill can become nonstop fun for an otter.

FL parents treat life in much the same way. They love to gather their friends and their children together and talk, talk, talk. In many ways, they're a party waiting to happen! With their children, they're quick to ask about their day, and they love to get into long discussions with them. They're optimistic and good motivators, and even if they do tend to forget the food and leave two hours late for a family camping trip, they'll have fun when they get there.

Remember how each pattern has strengths and weaknesses? While an FL parent is very encouraging and motivating to children, he can also do things that can lower his children's worth. One common problem is saying yes to so many other people and opportunities for work or play that there isn't any time left for the kids. Saying no is a skill FL parents need to learn. Even if it's only to a second piece of pie, they should make it a habit to say no to at least one thing a day.

FL parents can stray into another trap. In the book of Proverbs, we are told, "In the multitude of words sin is not lacking."[3] In their excitement to tell a story or relate some fact, sometimes FL parents can bend a story or slip in a "fact" here or there. In their need to be liked by others, instead of telling someone "I'm too busy," they'll stay up all night to get a project done and then be too tired to spend time with their families. Children (or spouses) who live with this can become frustrated at times, feeling they are number three or four (or seven or eight) on the list of priorities.

How can FL parents use their natural bent to build value into their children?

• By using their extensive network of friends and contacts to meet their children's (or mate's) needs.

• By showing enthusiasm over things their children (or spouse) accomplish.

• By structuring and initiating fun times and experiences that build family unity.

How can their strengths be pushed into weaknesses?

• By allowing their poor control of time to cost them time with the one group who "has to love them"—their family.

• By saying yes to things they know they need to say no to.

• By wanting too much to be liked by their children and failing to be firm with them as a result (particularly if they tend to have little of the Take-Charge parents' traits).

THE GIFT OF HONOR

Are You a Loyal-Friend Lisa (or Larry)?

Parents like Loyal-Friend (LF) Lisas and Larrys usually don't have as many friends as Fun-Loving parents, but the friendships they do have are much deeper. While Fun-Loving parents tend to know hundreds of people one-inch deep, Loyal-Friend parents have a deep desire to know a handful of people in depth. Not only that, but LF parents are incredibly loyal to their children, spouses, or friends. Of all the different kinds of parents, LF's can absorb or listen to tremendous amounts of pain or hurt when it involves the family or a close friend.

LF parents would rather stay home with their children than spend every night at the movies. They are excellent listeners and are empathetic when their children share hurts. They're good at calming things down when little Sammy is screaming that he's bleeding to death because of the scratch on his knee. And wherever they live—in a one-room apartment or a twelve-room mansion—their home reflects a warmth and a "This is home" feeling.

Just as we've seen in other parenting patterns, LF parents can do things by stressing their natural strengths to an extreme that can lower their children's worth. For example, their love for a stable, steady environment can make changes hard to take. Particularly if a child (or a spouse) is a Take-Charge or Fun-Loving person, things are going to change every day! And that leads to the next strength of an LF parent that can be pushed into a weakness.

Loyalty is unquestionably a tremendous quality. Yet sometimes LF parents will listen to another person's hurt so long and so intently that they never leave time to share their own hurts and needs. They tend to be very sensitive to their children's pain, but they also need to allow them room to grow up and not stay in the nest long after their wings need to be exercised. And as we note in the chapters on the dark side of family loyalties, sometimes being lovingly loyal means not only listening and hoping problems will work out, but (gasp!) confronting them as well.

How can LF parents use their natural bent to build value into their children?

• By using their excellent listening skills to demonstrate interest in what their child (or spouse) is saying.

• By modeling depth of communication instead of just flippant talk.

• By showing a commitment to each family member that in and of itself builds value in their loved ones.

How can they keep their strengths from being pushed into weaknesses?

• By learning that change represents an opportunity for growth instead of just a reason for concern.

• By taking risks to express their own hurts and needs instead of letting them pile up.

• By doing one thing a week (going to Bible study, having lunch with a friend, taking time alone to shop, reading a book of interest) that fills their emotional tank, which they so readily empty for others.

Are You a Let's-Be-Right Rita (or Randy)?

Fun-Loving parents ask, "Are we having fun yet?" *Let's-Be-Right (LBR) parents* ask, "Are we following the directions correctly yet?" If you lean toward being "right" and doing things by the book in everything you do, from the minute you find out you're pregnant (or your wife is), you've qualified as a genuine LBR person. Now that you're going to be a parent, you'll need to schedule the *right* number of doctor visits; take the *right* prenatal vitamins (are generic brands really as good as the others?); eat only the *right* things and avoid all the junk food the Fun-Loving parent sneaks on the side; and make sure you read the latest research about the *right* color to paint the nursery for a newborn.

Accuracy is an LBR parent's trademark, and her house, office, and children's rooms reflect that fact. She does a tremendous job of setting and keeping boundaries for herself and her children, but those boundaries can sometimes shift over to the rigid side.

A tremendous strength of LBR parents is their consistency and their "quality control" tendencies. Like Loyal-Friend parents, they'll be at the party when the invitation says, or when they think it is the "correct" time to be there. If a child has a big paper coming up in school or transportation has to be worked out between soccer practice and music lessons, you can be sure it'll be done right and on time.

LBR moms and dads give children orderliness and predictability that build their security and worth. However, like each of the parenting styles we've looked at, this one also can use natural strengths to drop a child's worth.

Pushed to an extreme, LBR parents' critical thinking and attention to detail can move into legalism and unhealthy perfectionism. Expecting their children or themselves to be perfect can add burdens instead of building worth. Fear of doing something wrong (like not reading this chapter correctly) and damaging their children for life can paralyze them and keep them from doing anything at all. Finally, when problems come or they get mad at their children (or spouse), they can step back several paces to avoid the pain instead of facing the anger or hurt and dealing with it.

How can LBR parents use their natural bent to build worth into their children?

• By providing a careful, predictable environment that encourages stability.

• By being diplomatic when an argument breaks out between the children and using logical thinking to straighten things out.

• By teaching their children that doing things correctly and working heartily unto the Lord can give them a sense of quality and accomplishment (and keeps them from having to do it again!).

How can these parents' strengths be kept from being pushed to an extreme?

• By seeing to it that "deep" cleaning, keeping the house in order, and spending the day "according to plan" don't get put ahead of taking time to play and talk with a child (or spouse).

• By keeping in mind that they can become very stern critics of the same people they once felt had so many positive qualities (and nine times out of ten still do).

• By facing up to conflict when it's necessary instead of avoiding it.

So far, we've looked at four different parenting types, each of which can build value into a child (or lower it if strengths get pushed to an extreme). As you looked over this list, perhaps you could easily pick yourself out, or you may have seen more than one pattern that describes you.

Some personality experts say that people are one "type" only or that certain types are totally incompatible with each other. We don't agree. We feel this puts too tight a label on people who are each tremendously complex. For example, we've seen a mother who was primarily a Fun-Loving Freda also have strong Let's-Be-Right Rita tendencies. We've seen a father who 90 percent of the time was a Loyal-Friend Larry become a Take-Charge Charlie at home the 10 percent of the time when his boss put him under extra pressure at work.

We feel that every parent has within himself or herself the capacity to develop and demonstrate each parenting style. Perhaps you've already seen this in yourself. Have you seen your parenting style change with the arrival of a new child or when your child reached a certain age?

To be able to build value in children throughout their lives, parents need to develop positive aspects of each parenting type. With toddlers who don't have the judgment yet to stay away from certain things, quick responses and take-charge characteristics are important. What grade-schooler doesn't need the nonstop entertainment a fun-loving parent can provide? Could a parent ever have enough loyal-friend patience and listening skills when dealing with an adolescent? And for children of any age, let's-be-right training can help them follow God's Word and stay on a positive path.

Wouldn't it be great if we could take the best of every personality bent and mold it into our lives? We have a model for that, you know. The better we know our heavenly Father, the more we'll see the incredible balance and maturity in the way He treats His children.

COMBINING THE BEST

With His disciples, Jesus put each parenting style into
practice. Can you think of ways in which He treated them
with take-charge tendencies? How about telling Peter to get
behind Him, standing up for the disciples when they were
challenged by the religious leaders, directing their ministry
and mission, and setting His face "like a flint"[4] to go to the
cross for them?

The Savior of the world modeled fun-loving characteristics to His disciples. Where was the first place He took
them? To a wedding. What was He constantly accused of
by the Pharisees? Being "a glutton and a winebibber."[5] He
talked with the "sinners" at length, and He often mingled
with crowds of needy people.

While Jesus felt compassion for the crowds He went
amongst, He also modeled depth in relationships with His
disciples. Could there ever be a better, more loyal friend to
sinners than our Lord? Within the disciples, there was an
inner circle of three. Within that circle, He had an even
deeper relationship with the "beloved disciple." Most intimate of all was His relationship with the Father, as seen in
the times—even hours before dawn—when He drew away
to enjoy that intimacy. Loyalty marked our Savior's life, a
loyalty that led all the way to the cross and beyond.

Can anyone convict Jesus of doing wrong? As long as He
was with His disciples, He demonstrated to them and called
on them to follow God's Word, which could guide and free
them. His carefully worded answers to the disciples and
every life He touched reflected a quality moment.

Each style of person, each style of parent can be seen in
our Lord. It should be seen in our lives as well. Most
incredible of all, He can give us the inner desire and strength
to build the best aspects of each style into our own parenting patterns.

TAKING THE NEXT STEP

Why not make a study of positive traits from each parenting style that you can build into your life? Choose one trait from each of the four you especially want to work on in the next six weeks, and ask your spouse or a close friend to hold you accountable at the end of that time.

We would also encourage you to take the time to explain to your children which parenting type you are most like today and admit to them your strengths and weaknesses. With just a little effort, you can help them identify their personal bent and see how their strengths make them special and valuable parts of your family.

If you find that in a family of four, each of you has a different pattern that predominates, don't lose heart. Each of you can make a decision to build balance into your life and develop the best from each bent.

Finally, don't crush or bend a child into a different pattern simply because you're most comfortable with your own pattern. You'll probably lean in one direction, but you can learn to shift, bend, and still keep your and your children's worth and identity intact.

Wise men and women seek wisdom and understanding.[6] Deepening your understanding about your own parenting strengths can help you live wisely with your children. In this third aspect of honor, you can find a key to opening each child's heart, filling it with love and self-worth. You can also find new value in yourself and the way God created you and wants you to develop.

Now that you're better aware of your parenting strengths and style, you can use this information and your individual bent to help you personally apply the principles in this book. And in particular, understanding yourself better can help you keep your home in a healthy balance, which is the next aspect of honor.

CHAPTER SEVEN

Providing a Healthy Balance in Our Homes: Part 1

It was two days before my (Gary's) fourteenth birthday when I paid a steep price for losing my balance. All my friends had been urging me to try to walk across a thin pine tree that had fallen across a deep, narrow ravine—a feat we called the suicide walk.

It really didn't look that difficult. All I had to do was keep my eyes glued to the end of the tree, walk a straight line, and not look down at the trees and razor-sharp rocks below. My first few steps across the fallen tree were confident, but my friends stopped cheering when they saw me lose my confidence, then my balance, and fall nearly twenty feet onto an old oak tree down below. Thankfully, that tree broke my fall and perhaps saved my life. But because of the impact when I hit, I was badly shaken and had a number of deep cuts and bruises.

It's not always easy to keep things in balance, even in a home, but in some cases it's extremely important. We're not trying to panic you by making you think your home is precariously perched. However, it's important for you to understand two crucial elements in building a high sense of value in your children that flow out of your decision to honor them—elements you need to work at keeping in balance. If a home is shifted too far in either direction, major problems can result.

These two important elements are (1) meeting their need

to belong while (2) easing them into separateness and independence. Let's look at each element and how it can provide lifelong help to children.

BUILDING ON BALANCE

There's an old story about two young children who were standing on the corner, bragging about who had moved from state to state the most. One little boy said, "My family has moved three times in the last three years."

"Hey!" said the other little boy. "That's nothing. My parents have moved five times this year—and I found them every time!" It's safe to say that this second boy came from a home without a strong sense of belonging.

Meeting a Child's Need to Belong

Belonging is the need each person has to feel a special, needed, and important part of the family. It's a feeling that we fit in with our parents and our brothers and sisters and that our contribution to the family is valued. It's knowing that we were planned (even if our timing was a surprise) instead of being an accident that somehow showed up to disrupt the family. Even more, it's knowing that God Himself designed our button nose or curly hair. (See Job 31:15; Psalm 119:73.)

Children who grow up with a strong sense of belonging gain ground on those who don't. The seeds of acceptance that are sown in children who feel they belong will bear fruit in giving them the ability to give and receive love and acceptance later in life.

Take Judy, for example. Although she missed out on belonging in her own home, it was served at every meal with her grandparents.

Judy grew up in a home where her parents showed little love and acceptance. Not only that, but as the youngest child of six, she also had to constantly put up with being teased by her brothers and sisters. If it wasn't her scraggly hair or her turned-up nose they made fun of, they loved to lie to the neighborhood children and tell them their parents found Judy when she was a baby abandoned in a vacant lot—and they were ready to send her back!

Yet in spite of this, Judy grew up feeling very special and valuable. Why? As she thought back, she realized it was the hours she spent in her *grandparents' home* that had molded her sense of belonging. Her grandparents lived just a few houses down from her family as she was growing up. Her grandfather was a retired carpenter, and her grandmother had the best lap to sit on for miles around. Every day after school, she would run into her grandparents' home for a cookie or snack before heading home. And every day she would gain a gift—a sense of belonging—even sweeter than the chocolate-chip cookies she would devour.

When her parents were too busy to listen, Grandma and Grandpa had nothing but time. When there was a problem with another girl at school, she received counsel, not an impatient lecture. When Judy was feeling hurt or discouraged, Grandma would cradle Judy's head in her lap and gently stroke her hair as she spoke loving, comforting words and sounds like "Mmmmmm" and "My, my" and "Bless your poor little heart." Judy even received reassurance from her grandparents that her parents and brothers and sisters really did love and value her. They just didn't know how to show it.

Today, Judy has one of the best marriages we know, and it didn't come from a vacuum. It came from loving grandparents who blessed her with a sense of belonging. And she, in turn, is blessing her children in the same way.

Meeting a Child's Need for Separateness

On the other side of the coin is separateness, the need each person has to feel he can accomplish things on his own, that he has unique skills and talents within the family. This is a concept that Kevin, as an identical twin, had to come to grips with. Being an identical twin brought Kevin a good deal of attention. With a carbon copy walking beside him, he felt little need to develop a uniquely individual identity in dealing with others—that is, until his brother decided to leave home to attend a military academy.

When we first saw Kevin in counseling, he was going through an intense time of depression. Alone for the first time, he felt abandoned and unprepared to face others. As long as his brother was present, he knew exactly how to act. But now that he had to make friends, set his own schedule, and make decisions without consulting his brother, he felt at a loss about where to begin.

> On the other side of the coin is separateness, the need each person has to feel he can accomplish things on his own, that he has unique skills and talents within the family.

Children who grow up without a healthy independence from their parents or siblings are in trouble. Procrastination, mood swings, difficulty in maintaining intimate relationships, problems with getting and staying motivated, and a deep-seated fear of being alone often hold them back from becoming all that God intends them to be.

In each household, there's a need for individual expression as well as for a strong sense of belonging. Both concepts need to be present in children if they are to take off and grow. Although these factors may look like irreconcilable extremes, each provides a sense of balance to the other.

It would be wonderful if every home perfectly balanced these two elements. However, that's not always the case. Some homes take a perfectly good family trait and push it to an unhealthy extreme.

PUSHING FAMILY STRENGTHS TO EXTREMES

The Taylors have a real strength in their family. They love to kid and joke with one another. Humor is often an important part of a close-knit home, but pushed to an extreme, it can become anything but funny.

Mary is the oldest daughter in the family, and in spite of her sensitivity to her weight problem, she knows that the next fat-girl joke is right around the corner. Like the day she wore a new red-white-and-blue dress for the first time and her sister announced at the dinner table, "Hey, everybody, did you notice Mary's new dress? Mary and I were standing on the corner today, and somebody came up and tried to mail a letter in her." Ha, ha, ha.

Even the parents get into the act of making fun of each other. Take the last time they went to the airport. As they pulled up to the terminal, a skycap asked, "Take your bag, mister?"

"No thanks," Mr. Taylor said. "She can walk!" Ha, ha, ha.

When humor is pushed to an extreme, soon the only safe conversations are shallow ones. If we cover all of life with humor, we are also covering over wells of important feelings and emotions that need to be expressed. Family members need to be able to share tears of sorrow as well as tears of joy.

A similar thing happens in homes that push separateness and belonging too far. Without a doubt, each is a family strength. However, a family can become so strong in one area that it throws the family off balance in another. That's exactly what happened to Joan.

When Belonging Is Shifted to an Extreme

Joan's family stressed belonging . . . and stressed it . . . and stressed it! To outsiders, this emphasis may have passed for an unusually strong sense of togetherness, but to Joan, it meant being trapped in a web of manipulation that she felt powerless to cut through.

Joan participated in home schooling long before it was

fashionable to do so. Her parents' decision was made not
from a fear of what was being taught in public schools but
from a fear of the influence outsiders might have on her.
Joan's only friends were her brothers and sisters, and they
were all strictly forbidden from playing with the "inferior"
neighborhood children.

Even in high school, when she was allowed to attend the
public school, she was expected to come home immediately
after class. "After all, there are so many things we have to
do as a family, there just isn't time for all those 'other'
people." That was the typical response to any request she
would make to take part in outside activities.

Her parents' constant discouragement of participation with
her peers did much to deepen Joan's shyness, and she
found herself withdrawn and fearful of other teen-agers at
school. Hearing the other girls talk about a slumber party
might bring pains of loneliness, but an even greater fear of
being away from her family for the night pushed loneliness
aside.

Together with her parents, Joan shouted out the message,
"We only have time for each other!" Alone at night she
whispered, "Why don't I fit in with others outside my
family?"

Today, as an insecure twenty-nine-year-old, Joan lacks
any real confidence that she can exist outside her family
context. She has held several jobs and has spent a short
stint at a community college. Yet every time she encounters
trials or interpersonal struggles, she either quits her job or
ends a relationship—and draws further back into a faltering
coexistence with her parents.

Angry with them for her lack of healthy independence,
she pouts and broods when she's at their house. But afraid
of alienating her only source of acceptance, she's unwilling to give up the stifling relationship she has with her
parents. While she often dreams of a Prince Charming who
will ride up and take her away, she always awakens to
a king and queen who hold her heart in a dishonoring
home.

In this home, the family strength of belonging has been

taken so far to the extreme that it has thrown Joan's life out of balance. A very similar result came about in George's home, where separateness was pushed to an extreme.

When Separateness Is Pushed to an Extreme

George came from a strong ethnic background. His parents walked off the boat and right into work at a shoe repair business. In the almost thirty-five years since then, they have worked day and night. The same thing was expected of each of the children who came along. "Get yourself up, and get to work!" the kids heard often.

At forty-three years of age, George can never remember his parents' telling him they loved him or were proud of him. What he remembers clearly are the times he was told he could make it on his own or he would never make it at all.

He vividly recalls one incident. When he was a boy, his family lived in a neighborhood where they were the only ones from their ethnic background. One day, three older boys followed him home from school, taunting him about his accent. When George said something cutting back to them, they gave him a terrible beating and left him lying in the street.

George's head and face throbbed with pain as he lay there sobbing and fighting for breath. When he was finally able to roll onto his side, he looked up and saw his father standing on their front porch only yards away. He had been standing there the whole time.

"Why," George cried, "why didn't you help me?"

Before walking back into the house, his father told him, "Let it be a lesson to you. No one can fight your battles for you."

In some ways, having to stand up for himself did make George stronger. He got much better at fighting and developed an independent spirit that he took on to college and the business world. The only problem was that he took that same "stand alone" attitude into his marriage.

Growing up with separateness and an exaggerated emphasis on being self-sufficient, he longed for the love and warmth he saw in his wife during their courtship. However, feeling comfortable only with separateness, he didn't know how to give or receive that love, and soon his callousness had strained their marriage to the breaking point. George could stand on his own two feet, all right. What he couldn't do was put his arms around anyone else, including his wife and children.

Take separateness to an extreme and you have the potential to produce the loneliest people in the world. Nothing is more pitiful than watching a thirsty man who lies with fresh water just out of reach. Watching someone who is supremely *independent* but who can never be *interdependent* inspires just as much compassion.

Always longing to hear words of love and acceptance, he will stiff-arm those very words if they finally come his way. Even though he knows intellectually that he needs to verbalize his love for his family, he's never able to relinquish the pride wrapped around his independence.

When such people become Christians, watch how their drive will often cause them to strive for teaching, counseling, or leadership positions in the church or parachurch organizations. In some cases, it's just their natural drive that's surfacing. But in many others, the safest place to hide in a room where people are asking questions or discussing relationships is to be the one leading the discussion.

SPARKS CAN FLY WHEN EAST MEETS WEST

What happens when someone who grows up in a home that stresses separateness to an extreme meets someone who comes from a home just as committed to belonging? Oftentimes, it's called marriage!

It's sometimes said that two twenty-year-olds marry to make one forty-year-old. That was almost too true for Joan and Norm. When Joan looked at Norm, his independence and ability to make decisions apart from his family seemed terrific. She came from a home where the family members were so tied together that she had never felt any freedom of choice in any decision she ever made. In Norm she saw the independence she longed for.

Norm was just as taken with Joan. He couldn't believe how close her family was. She was carrying a full load of classes at school and working part-time, and she still made time to call her mother two or three times every day. Norm hadn't even bothered to call home at Thanksgiving. But then no one from home had tried to call him either.

In Joan, Norm saw a side of himself he knew was lacking. If anyone could make him feel complete and acceptable, she had to be the expert on belonging. The reverse was true for Joan. She saw in Norm the embodiment of strength to help her stand apart from her family. He would supply the courage she had never been able to muster to make the change. In her eyes, he was an Olympic medalist or an All-American in the field of separateness.

But a funny thing happened on the way home from the altar. What was so stimulating in their courtship became killing in their marriage. Norm spent almost every waking moment badgering Joan to meet his needs for acceptance. He kept looking for more and more depth in their relationship, more and more touching and physical closeness, and grew impatient and irritable if they weren't actively involved in Bible study, marriage group, or something else that would help them "become intimate."

On the other hand, Joan had already had twenty years of over-involvement with her family, and she reacted to Norm's calls for closeness by drawing away. For the first time in her young life she was on her own. Even the thought of getting deeply intimate with Norm was emotionally like going back inside a windowless classroom to study state government after getting to run outside on a beautiful spring day.

Instead of the strength she bargained for, Joan saw only Norm's emotional weakness and vulnerability. Instead of the warmth that had enraptured him, Norm thought he had been duped into marrying a defiant, uncaring, independent Joan.

Both Norm and Joan got all they were looking for in a marriage partner—and less. Going into marriage with their private lives tilted to one extreme or the other left little middle ground on which to build a lasting marriage. It was only after they began to individually balance their lives and to understand what unhealthy extremes they had reached that Norm had the freedom to let go of his stranglehold on her and give her room to grow, while Joan was able to draw closer to her husband.

People have always been fascinated by extremes. That's part of what pushed them to explore the polar regions and outer space. However, maintaining a healthy marriage or raising children is a different matter. Homes shifted to an extreme may be interesting to visit, but they instill low value in those who live there. Whether belonging is taken to an extreme or separateness is way out of balance, children go from such homes only half-prepared to be successful in relationships.

A BIBLICAL BALANCE POINT

Where do we go to find an example of someone who balanced separateness and belonging in intimate relationships? We can look at the Master Lover and Equipper, for Jesus' relationship with the disciples pictures just such a balance.

Think of all the times and ways He communicated to the disciples before His death, resurrection, and ascension that they were secure in His love for them. In conversations with the disciples, standing near or in private times with them alone, He built in an unmistakable sense of attachment to each of His own with statements like these:

> Do not worry, saying, "What shall we eat?" or "What shall we drink?" or "What shall we wear?" . . . But seek first the kingdom of God and His righteousness, and all these things shall be added to you (Matthew 6:31, 33).

> My sheep hear My voice, and I know them . . . I give them eternal life, and they shall never perish; neither

97

shall anyone snatch them out of My hand (John 10:27–28).

Let not your heart be troubled; you believe in God, believe also in Me. . . . I go to prepare a place for you. And if I go and prepare a place for you, I will come again and receive you to Myself (John 14:1–3).

And I will pray to the Father, and He will give you another Helper, that He may abide with you forever, . . . He dwells with you and will be in you. I will not leave you orphans (John 14:16–18).

The disciples would always be able to rest in their Savior's love, yet they were also given wings and the encouragement to carry a message of hope beyond the confines of their company. In fact, they were sent out time and again to carry the message of their King.

And He called the twelve to Him, and began to send them out two by two (Mark 6:7).

Behold, I send you out as sheep in the midst of wolves (Matthew 10:16).

Even on His last night with the disciples, Jesus comforted them with His love. Yet He also made it clear that they would have His Spirit, though not His physical presence, to guide them after that night. He said, "I tell you the truth. It is to your advantage that I go away; for if I do not go away, the Helper will not come to you; but if I depart, I will send Him to you" (John 16:7).

The disciples knew they were secure in their relationship with Christ, but they also knew it was natural and right to leave the mountaintop and go into the trenches with hurting people. Isn't it interesting how both aspects combined to mold the disciples into a force that changed the world? If they had been given a sense of belonging through the security of their relationship with Him but had never been encouraged to go out from their spiritual family, you wouldn't be reading a Christian book today. On the other hand, they would never have been able to stand fast and face the hardships they did in spreading the gospel without knowing they were eternally secure in God's love.

How does all this relate to parents' trying to honor their children by building worth and value into their lives? For three years, our Lord blended a message of love and acceptance with the encouragement to His disciples to take their faith to others outside their immediate circle. For parents, much the same task exists today.

Build in a strong sense of belonging, and your children will go away from home emotionally secure and less susceptible to peer pressure. Balance it by easing them into healthy independence, and you've given them both warmth and wings.

CHAPTER EIGHT

Providing a Healthy Balance in Our Homes: Part 2

What marks a home as a place where belonging takes root and grows? How can you provide a healthy separateness for your children without pushing them out of the nest too soon? In this chapter, we'll look at both aspects of keeping a home in balance, beginning with a look at belonging. When it comes to helping a child feel he belongs, we've found five marks that surface time and again as we interview families all across the country.

BUILDING BELONGING IN A CHILD'S LIFE

1. We Build Belonging By Expressing Praise and Appreciation.

Praising others or receiving their praise has a number of incredible by-products, including feelings of acceptance and belonging. Researchers have found this to be true even when people knew the nice things being said about them *weren't true*.

One study was conducted using two groups of clothing salesclerks. The two groups carried the same items, but their approaches to customers were very different. One group of clerks would speak only when spoken to and even then kept conversation to a minimum. The other salesmen did their best to make pleasing comments: "Is this dress for your sister?" to a young matron shopping with her nineteen-year-old daughter, or "I hope you know you're looking great today!"

Do you know what they found after interviewing shoppers and looking at sales in the two groups? Even when people knew they were being buttered up or unjustly flattered, they tended to think more highly of and buy more from the salesmen who unjustly praised them! They also said they would rather frequent the store where they were complimented, even if it was only flattery.[1]

Within a family, think how much greater the effect of legitimate praise can have on your loved ones. Children who grow up hearing words of thanks and appreciation often feel special and part of the group. One family we know has made this principle into an art—literally.

There's a tradition in the Keefer family that is everybody's favorite. Three months before Christmas, each person reaches into a hat and pulls out the name of some other family member. On the big day, handmade artistic creations that represent something special about the recipients are exchanged. From stick figures to oil paintings, each year some new art form takes shape. After Christmas, these artworks go into the Keefer Museum of Very Valuable People (better known as the wall in Dad's workshop).

This tradition was started by Mr. Keefer. For years he struggled with being able to express words of love and approval to his children. He knew he should, but he didn't find it easy to do. So, he spent hours in his workshop making special presents for each child. In giving his handmade gifts and telling each child the significance of the gift, he learned to more freely express his love and appreciation to his children.

What began as a liability in being able to express appreciation only through handmade gifts has been turned into a meaningful tradition. Each Christmas each child receives a special present and hears a story about his or her special value in front of the rest of the family.

Expressing genuine appreciation for your children is one

way you build feelings of belonging into their lives. It can take so little time, yet it helps your children leave home feeling loved.

2. We Build Belonging through Listening.

In study after study, the healthiest families are those who score high in the area of listening. In fact, listening may be one of the healthiest things we can do.

In a study at Johns Hopkins Medical School, cardiac patients are being taught the life-saving skill of how to listen to others![2] The medical researchers have found that a common denominator in many who suffered a heart attack was an inability or unwillingness to actively listen to others.

While using a machine that continuously monitored a person's blood pressure, they noticed an unusual happening. Every time a patient spoke to someone else—without exception—his blood pressure went up. Whenever a person took the time to listen to someone else, however, *his heartbeat and blood pressure went down*.

In some patients, even though their words sounded calm when they were talking, blood pressure climbed up into the danger zone for heart attacks. It may be hard to believe, but some patients actually talked so much and listened so little that it was a life-and-death problem![3]

We're not saying that listening to your children is a matter of life and death (even though the Scriptures do tell us that 'life and death are in the power of the tongue'),[4] but it *is* emotionally and physically healthy for them and you. It also deepens their sense of belonging.

Joe Bayly was a godly man who recently went home to be with the Lord. During his lifetime, he and his wife had the burden of seeing three of their sons die due to accident or illness. In his excellent book *The Last Thing We Talk About*, Joe gave an example of the way that simply listening to people can bond us to them.

After the death of our second son, I can remember two visits from people quite vividly.

One person came into the room, loudly talking about

how "special" we were to God because this had hap-
pened to us and how God must have known in advance
that we had the strength to handle this tragedy. He
recited several Bible verses and then went out as loudly
as he had come in. I felt unmoved, almost angry and
glad he had gone.

Then another friend came in. He just came over and
sat down beside me. He took my hand. He listened. He
prayed briefly, and he left quietly. I was moved. I was
comforted. I wished he hadn't had to leave.[5]

Most of us are far better lecturers than we are listeners.
Even when we do listen, it's often just a pause between
bursts of what's really important—what *we* have to say!
Yet if children are to know that they are important, we
need to show them by listening to them.

Be aware of this. The "Smalley-Trent Axiom of Communication" states, "The opportunity to listen to your children is directly proportional to the interest of the television
program you are watching or book you are reading." In
other words, the more interesting the program or the more
exciting the plot of the book, the more likely that that will
be the very time your children want to talk!

We know you can't drop everything every time your
children want to share something with you. But if you close
the door to communication too many times, before long you
won't have to worry about shutting it at all. They will quit
sharing with you even when you plead with them to talk to
you.

I (John) remember a comment my mother would make
repeatedly to her kids during our teen-age years. Because
of her health problems, she would often have to go to bed
quite early. But nearly every night, before retiring she would
say, "Just wake me up if you boys want to talk about
something. I can always go back to sleep, but I can't
always talk with you."

Do you know what my twin brother and I used to do
almost every weekend after getting home from our dates or
a ball game in high school? You guessed it. We'd walk into
our mother's room, flop down on the bed on either side of

her, wake her up, and sometimes talk for hours about our dates, problems, dreams, goals, or life in general.

During a period of time in our teen-age years when many parents would love to be able to know what their children were thinking and doing, Mother knew many things in detail, largely because she built a sense of belonging in our lives by having an open-door policy when it came to listening.

3. We Build Belonging By Providing a Well-Defined Purpose for the Home.

Have you ever seen a business that's struggling? In many cases, such companies are guided by yesterday's actions or today's crisis instead of a clear purpose or plan. Employees can sense when a business is pointed in the right direction or when its leadership is simply navigating by the seat of its pants.

The same thing is true with a team. Our good friend Norm Evans, a former member of two of the Miami Dolphins' Super Bowl teams, gave us some valuable insight into winning teams and winning families. Much of what Norm taught us we see consistently in healthy families across America.

Norm told us the story of what it was like when Don Shula took over as the Dolphins' head coach. The year before Shula came, the team had 2 wins and 10 losses and was a struggling expansion franchise. But at the first team meeting he had with his players, the new coach told them, "Men, our goal for the year is to be 10–2."

Some team members chuckled to themselves, but Shula went on to explain how this could take place. "We're going to practice four times a day, every day, to get ready for the games on Sunday. Not only that, but you'll learn everything there is to know about the player across from you by the end of the week. You'll have a plan and will have practiced that plan until you're 100 percent ready for the game on Sunday."

Their record that year was 10–2, and the next year they were 13–0 and won the Super Bowl. Don Shula is now the winningest active head coach in the NFL for good reason.

He has a clear purpose behind his methods and a plan for his team, and they practice it.

What's important to a successful business or sports team is also important in a close-knit home. As a family, we (the Smalleys) sat down with each of our children and set up a plan in our home that included three basics: honoring God, honoring each other, and honoring His creation. Then every night for three years while they were in grade school, we talked for a few minutes at the dinner table about how each of us was doing individually and as a family in these three areas.

As Norma and I recall the things that have positively affected our children, those three years of having a clear plan and practicing it each night have been a significant factor in helping each child mature and in keeping us together as a close-knit team. Not every football team reaches the Super Bowl, and not every family is a "Super Bowl" family. But we want at least to win more than we lose! And to do so, we all need a family plan we can practice daily in our homes.

God's Word is the blueprint for a successful life and family. Putting His Word into a practical plan of action parents can follow (in this case, understanding and applying seven aspects of honoring loved ones) is one of our main ministry goals.[6]

Children can sense whether there's a clear purpose or plan in their home or there's simply a collection of rules that are unrelated and unclear. Having a plan and practicing it can be an important way to encourage healthy independence in children. But for now, let's look at a fourth way in which we can build belonging in our children.

4. We Build Belonging By Making Sure Each Person Feels a Shared Burden for the Others.

Principles that surround our spiritual family can also enrich our natural family. In a church struggling with divisions and a lack of unity, the apostle Paul offered a word picture that illustrates the importance of family unity. Likening different Christians to different parts of the body, he said,

"And if one member [like a hand or an eye] suffers, all the members suffer with it; or if one member is honored, all the members rejoice with it" (1 Corinthians 12:26).

One thing that stands out in the healthiest families we see is this type of shared burden for one another. If Daughter Jane is hurting, everyone comes alongside her to provide encouragement and support. If Son David is given a promotion at work, the success is shared with everyone.

How can parents build a sense of unity in their families, especially when they have healthy, average kids who by nature would rather fight with one another than eat? One thing I (Gary) have found that has drawn us into unity as a family more than any other is experiencing a trial together. Again, I'm not advocating *creating* trials. The book of James tells us that trials will come naturally. In our home, all we need to do is plan a family get-together, and something is bound to go wrong and draw us into unity as a result. Let me explain what I mean.

Several years ago, when the children were still in grade school, we decided to load up our mobile home and head to Colorado for a vacation. The trip proved to be uneventful until one particularly steep grade. Suddenly, as I looked down on the dash, I could see the temperature reading was "Hot!"

The kids looked forward to any reason for a stop, so as soon as I pulled the mobile home over to the side of the road, they jumped out and started running all over the place. As if it weren't enough that we were afraid they would run out into the highway and get hit, our older son, Greg, had the great idea of drop-kicking a can of oil that he found.

As if guided by a NASA radar system, the half-full can of oil flew high in the air and landed directly on the head of our younger son, Michael. He was drenched with oil from head to toe and got a big bump on his head.

I think you can picture the scene. The car is overheated. Greg is hiding because he knows he's in big trouble. Norma and our daughter, Kari, are crying because some of the oil got in Mike's eyes and they're afraid he'll go blind. Mike is crying because he's mad at Greg and because he can't see him to get revenge. I'm looking for some water to wash off the oil—and then it begins to rain!

As we all huddled in the mobile home, waiting for the car to cool down so we could take Mike to a doctor, no one said how great a family time it was or how unified we felt as a family. But once the trial was over (with no permanent damage to anything except the oil can), we've looked back on this near catastrophe a hundred times and laughed about it. As painful as they are when they happen, trials shared together can bond us and help us raise the value of our children.

5. We Build Belonging By Being Willing to Admit What the "Wise" Readily Acknowledge.

Of all the practical truths in the book of Proverbs, there are two simple instructions that can specifically help a parent build a sense of belonging in a child and raise his self-worth as a result: (1) the humble receive honor (Proverb 15:33) and (2) only the wise seek advice and correction for their ways (Proverb 1:7).

One of the hardest things for many parents to do is to admit to a child when they have made a mistake. For other parents, being open to receive legitimate correction from a child is even more difficult. In the Scriptures, however, the humble readily admit that they don't "know it all." They are open, teachable, willing to be corrected. You may think that saying "I'm sorry" or "I don't know" lowers your children's respect for you, but it does just the opposite. Children and others are drawn to people who are willing to admit they make mistakes and have flaws.

Dr. Charles Swindoll is one of our favorite pastors and Bible teachers, and we're not alone. His books and "Insight for Living" radio ministry have deeply affected thousands of men and women across the country, challenging them to grow deeper in the Christian life. What makes his ministry so effective? While there are certainly a number of good theological reasons, we believe it's because he's willing to be very honest and vulnerable about his successes and failures. It's hard to listen to someone who puts himself three levels above us. It's easy to relate to and be challenged by someone like Chuck Swindoll who lets us know he shares our struggles and has hurt where we hurt. The same things ring true for a parent.

It's humbling to say "I'm sorry" to your children, but it helps them to realize that you're honest with your weaknesses and that you have the feet of clay they see anyway! Early in life, children don't see many flaws in their parents. In most cases, until they are well into grade school, they look at parents as larger than life and often without fault. Yet the day will come when they begin to see your imperfections. And when they do, if you try to hide them or deny them, you lose ground in their eyes and teach them to deny problem areas in their lives. Being dishonest in this way can lower your children's self-worth, not raise it. By humbling yourself and even seeking correction, you can reverse that trend. Here's one example of how this has worked in my (Gary's) home.

Recently, my daughter Kari asked me to read several chapters of Proverbs with her that she had been studying in her Bible class in college. She had already marked up many of the verses, and as we read the chapters verse by verse, we stopped frequently and asked, "How do these verses match up with the way we're living our lives today?"

The first five verses we read instructed us that God wants us to search diligently and enthusiastically for His truth, even more than seeking after silver and gold. The next few verses spelled out specific attitudes and actions for those who would gain the skill of right living.

As we talked and evaluated our daily actions, Kari read one verse and mentioned that it was an area I needed to work on. I could tell after she said it that she didn't know whether she should have said it. She looked at me to see if I was upset or defensive and if she was in trouble! When she saw that I was open to correction, however—especially from my daughter—it helped her be that much more open and accepting of things she could work on in her own life.

After that time together, we both felt our love for each other grow stronger. We each had grown in our respect for the other because we could admit we don't "know it all" and we stand in need of correction at times like everyone else.

Add a willingness to receive correction to each of the other four ways to build belonging in children, and you have five key ingredients to raise your children's self-worth. And when children feel they truly belong, they are far better prepared to develop the second element you need to keep in balance in your home, which is a healthy separateness and independence.

PROVIDING HEALTHY SEPARATENESS

1. Ease Them into Independence.

The key to encouraging a healthy sense of separateness in children is easing them into independence. One noted family physician believes this begins way back when we're weaning them.

The Hebrew word for *weaned* is *gamal*, which means "to ripen."[7] The term implies a state of readiness. Weaning should mean not a loss of or a detachment from a relationship, but a state in which a child feels so full and so right that he or she is ready to take on other relationships. Listen to what Dr. William Sears has to say about children who are rushed into relationships and responsibilities before they're ready to handle them.

> *Weaning before his time of spiritual readiness may leave a child unfulfilled and not feeling right. A child who is weaned from any childhood relationships before his time, and is hurried into other relationships may perhaps rebel both inwardly and outwardly and show what I call, "diseases of unreadiness."*[8]

What are these "diseases"? Negative behaviors like out-of-balance aggressiveness, violent tantrums, and severe mood swings, to name a few. These are not the occasional tantrums or pouting of nearly any child; these are repeated negative patterns and behaviors from a hurried child.

In our experience with parents and children, we've observed that children of any age who are hurried into taking on too much independence too soon struggle in their relationships. Sometimes the death of a parent or a divorce forces a child to grow up "overnight." But if there is any way possible to do it, small steps toward independence are always the best.

2. Provide Children with Choices Appropriate to Their Ages.

David Elkind wrote a best-selling book titled *The Hurried Child*. He may have sold so many copies because so many "hurried children" ran out and bought it!

We live in an instant society today. Many people get upset if their hamburger and shake aren't ready by the time they drive the four car-lengths from the clown to the pickup window! The same thing holds true of many children.

In an incredibly complicated society, parents often expect their children to make sophisticated judgments without preparing them with wise counsel. Children didn't invent expensive designer jeans for four-year-olds, but parents buy them by the droves. It's not unusual for five- and six-year-old children to come to school wearing make-up because their parents are in a hurry for them to grow up. But is it healthy?

Just like you, we've walked by the mall and watched five- and six-year-olds walk out of R-rated movies with their parents. Their moms and dads expect them to handle the fastballs thrown at them in such films without an error.

For every parent who feels his child can handle R-rated movies or literature, we can give one hundred examples of children who could not and were hurt by them. Biblically, we see no reason why even a "mature" teen-ager or adult should view such material. At the very least, watching such films can lower a person's self-worth, and at worst, it can give them permission to dishonor God and act out dishonoring practices they have viewed or read about. Remember the biblical term "to wean"? It means we allow someone to ripen and mature before we expose him to decisions and responsibilities that require real discernment and judgment.

A tremendous privilege I (Gary) had in life was getting to spend a great deal of time with Corrie ten Boom in her later years. She is the one who encouraged me to use "word pictures" and "objects" every time I speak, and that's become a trademark of our ministry today. Her faith was forged in a loving Christian home and then tested and found true in a German concentration camp during World War II.

Corrie told me a story that she also recounted in her inspiring autobiography, *The Hiding Place*. When she was a little girl of six, riding on a train with her father, she looked out on a pastoral setting and saw cattle in the process of breeding. Out of curiosity, Corrie asked her father, "What are those animals doing?"

"Corrie," her father said, "everything has a proper time. When it's the right time for you to know, we'll have a talk, the two of us." That was all Corrie needed to know at the time, and a few years later, when the time was ripe, they did have that talk.

Building healthy separateness into children doesn't come at the expense of their losing their innocence. We know of one set of parents who let a college-aged boy (known to have a terrible reputation) take their thirteen-year-old daughter on an overnight camping trip with several non-Christian couples. Unfortunately, we then watched them regret their lack of courage to say no when she became pregnant out of wedlock. While permissiveness may prevail in some circles, it has nothing to do with the courage parents need to have to withhold things from their children until they are ready.

Understanding a child's readiness to accept choices and responsibilities is a key to helping him gain a healthy sense of separateness.

3. Set Goals for Their Going—and Practice and Review Those Goals.

Let's ask a few questions. What goals do you have for your child's "going"? What character traits would you like him or her to leave home with? How often do you sit down and talk about character strengths or areas that need to be developed with your child? What view of God and others is she carrying away from home every day?

Many of you are familiar with the verse that tells you to "train up a child in the way he should go, / And when he is old he will not depart from it" (Proverb 22:6). While the section referring to the child's remembering his early training often gets top billing, it's actually telling you to have a goal for the child's going! (Train him up in the way he should *go*.)

Each day you have a child in your home is a day you capture or lose in preparing him to go. Getting your child ready to leave home is a high calling. The character traits and degree of responsibility you see surfacing in your child today will be essentially what you see magnified in his life five years from now, or ten. This is also true of how successful he feels at standing apart from you and on his own two feet.

In a marriage, one aspect of genuine love involves preparing for the future, even for a time when one partner is no longer with the family. That's why you spend time setting up IRA's and pensions, making out a will and picking guardians for your children, and why both a husband and a wife should know about the family finances and how to handle them. The same care that goes into preparing for your own future should go into preparing your children for their future.

Like an unprepared widow who feels lost and directionless at the death of her spouse, a child whose parents set no goals for his going can be left just as unprepared to leave home. You need to ask yourself questions that can help you get him ready to go. These include questions like the following.

What can I teach my child about finances today that can help him feel capable to handle his own finances later? How about starting his own checking and savings accounts and making sure he learns the importance of tithing? It's also important to teach him today that being faithful with a little is God's criterion for being faithful with much. Also, look for everyday opportunities to build responsibility in this area. For example, if a child leaves his bicycle unlocked and it's stolen, instead of your buying him a new one, have him save his own money to replace it.

What can I do today to teach my child to make wise decisions? How about reading through Proverbs with him over the course of a summer or a school year and seeing how these wise principles stack up in everyday life? While you're reading it with him, you can take the time to point out specific verses that confirm right choices he has made in the past and help him analyze and learn from his mistakes in the present.

> Like an unprepared widow who feels lost and directionless at the death of her spouse, a child whose parents set no goals for his going can be left just as unprepared to leave home.

How can I learn to strengthen and develop his view of God before he leaves home? Many parents delegate what the child learns about the Lord to the church or a Christian school. Although these can be tremendous places of learning and spiritual encouragement, the knowledge he picks up can remain "head" knowledge instead of "heart" knowledge unless a parent sets spiritual goals at home. You should take the lead in helping your child learn to understand and apply the Scriptures. If he sees no crossover between what he learns at church and what occurs in his home, the Bible can become just another textbook relegated to a dusty bookshelf in years to come.

Developing and practicing a plan for his "going" in each of these major areas and others should begin when a child is in diapers. And it should continue each day that he's under your care. Getting a child ready to leave home in a healthy way involves more than giving him a pep talk before his high-school graduation and handing him a tuition check for college.

Parents who set no goals for their children's going actually dishonor them and leave them unprepared to face the challenges of real life. Parents who take time to develop a specific plan in this area honor their children by helping them become better prepared for their future. Even so, without a much-needed step, setting goals for when children leave home may not be enough.

A Much-Needed Step in Setting Goals for Their Going. Setting goals for their going is one way you can honor your children. However, to make sure these goals move from your mind and into their lives, don't forget a key ingredient, which is to be sure you *review* your plan periodically.

It is said in business that people do what you "inspect," not what you "expect." There is some truth to this when it comes to setting goals for your children's going as well. At the very least, we encourage parents to sit down together near each child's birthday each year and ask themselves how they are doing at implementing their goals for that child's going. They can ask questions like these: What have we seen in our child this year that reflects his increased love for and knowledge of God? How responsible has he been in carrying out chores or taking care of pets around the house? At school and at home, is he developing the ability to get along with others? How faithful has he been in giving to the Lord and managing his allowance or the money he's earned? Then plan a time to sit down with that child and praise him for his accomplishments, as well as to work together to set next year's goals.

Setting goals for your child's going and reviewing them each year (along with how well you did at encouraging and supporting those goals) is a tremendous way to ease a child into independence. If you need further help in setting a specific plan, we recommend two excellent books that go into detail in this area.[9]

It takes time to sit down with your child and set goals, but it certainly beats the alternative. If you aim at nothing in helping a child leave home in a healthy way, you're likely to hit it every time.

4. Promote Landmark Ages and Accomplishments.

Is there a "Hall of Honor" in your home? There should be. It doesn't have to be a hallway. A faded scrapbook will do just as nicely. Whether it's pictures you hang on the wall or ticket stubs you keep in a scrapbook, however, making special note of landmark accomplishments in your children's lives is a tremendous encouragement to them. Things to be honored are having their first dance recital; playing their first soccer game; graduating from grade school, high school, college, or trade school; turning a certain age; or winning a certain award. Making mention of milestones in children's lives frees them to go on to new and more difficult stages instead of freezing them in the uncertainty of their abilities.

We saw this very thing take place with a young woman we met on a plane recently. Betty looked every inch a cadet when we sat down next to her. In the course of a casual conversation, we discovered that she was flying home after graduating from one of the nation's military academies and receiving her pilot's wings.

"That must have been a tremendous time for you!" we said.

"It was. Well, it should have been," said Betty as she looked down at her lap. When we gently pressed her for further comment, she sighed and said, "All my life I've waited for my father to say he was proud of me. I knew in my heart it would happen yesterday. I just knew it. But it didn't. I know he's proud of me, but I would have given anything to hear it from him. I guess I'll just have to work as hard as I can to be a good pilot. Maybe then he'll say it."

Can you sense the search this poor girl is on? By failing to recognize significant milestones in children's growth and achievements, parents fail to give them a sense of accomplishment. Perhaps because he had never heard words of encouragement growing up, this father failed to pass them along to his daughter. And because of it, another person searches for a healthy feeling of separateness, an inner sense of completion that says, "I've finally accomplished something worthwhile. I finally stood on my own and did something I'm proud of and my parents are proud of.''

Keith Hernandez is one of baseball's top players. He is a lifetime .300 hitter who has won numerous Golden Glove awards for excellence in fielding. He's won a batting championship for having the highest average, the Most Valuable Player award in his league, and even the World Series. Yet with all his accomplishments, he has missed out on something crucially important to him—his father's acceptance and recognition that what he has accomplished is valuable. Listen to what he had to say in a very candid interview about his relationship with his father: "One day Keith asked his father, 'Dad, I have a lifetime .300 batting average. What more do you want?' His father replied, 'But someday you're going to look back and say, "I could have done more." ' "[10]

Gordon MacDonald, in his outstanding book *Ordering Your Private World,* points out that hurried adults and hurried children never "close the loop" on anything.[11] What he means is that they can never do anything well enough to prove to themselves or to their parents that they are finished with it. They always have to run faster, jump higher, try harder, all in an attempt to hear words of approval and acceptance. And even when they do hear them from parents, they rarely believe they can stop their frantic efforts.

In contrast to those who never feel a sense of recognition for milestone events or ages, we know of one family where just the opposite is true. Hank is a Christian education director who has world-class children. Each of his three daughters could be a poster child for someone who has grown up with a genuine sense of belonging and also developed a healthy sense of separateness from the family. What's this man's secret? When we asked each of the now-grown girls to tell us one thing their father did to instill a healthy sense of separateness in their lives, they all said the same thing: "my sixteen candle date with my father."

What is a "sixteen candle date"? Simply something a wise father did to mark a milestone in each daughter's life. And the only thing each girl had to "accomplish" before she spent this special time with Dad was to grow older.

When each daughter turned sixteen (and for two or three years before), Dad would mention little things about a special night out for the two of them. And while Old Testament parents marked a child's coming of age with a special ceremony of blessing, this father used an evening out to mark a special coming of age in his daughter's life.

From walking up to the door with a corsage in his hand, to going out for a special dinner at a fine restaurant, to presenting a handwritten wish list and a prayer list for this daughter and her family in years to come, he made it an evening none of the girls would ever forget. One daughter told us,

> *After my sixteen candle dinner with my father, I felt for the first time like I was really growing up. We talked about some of the responsibilities like dating and driving I had ahead of me, and it really helped me realize it was time to grow up.*

Make special mention of milestones in your children's growth and maturity, things they have reached by age or their best efforts, and you honor them by giving them a sense of accomplishment (closing the loop). This track record of acknowledged successes is something they can build on throughout their lives in serving the Lord and their families.

Your children may be eleven, eighteen, twenty-four, or forty-two, but you can still have a "sixteen candle date" with them. It's not the age that matters. Rather, what you say to them really makes the impact.

THE BLESSING OF A BALANCED HOME

We've looked at five ways to build a strong sense of belonging in our homes, and four ways in which we can ease our children into independence. Each aspect of a balanced home goes a long way toward making children feel valuable and secure, raising their self-worth as a result.

Honoring our own parents, helping our children find value in troubled times, discovering our own parenting strengths and style, and now uncovering the importance of keeping the home in balance—these four aspects of honor can help us develop a game plan for a winning family. They become even stronger when we add a fifth aspect of honor that was brought home to me when I (Gary) was a young boy.

As a child, I "fell into" one of the most fearful experiences of my life. Today, I realize it was only God's grace that helped me make it out alive. Looking back on that horror-filled afternoon, I can see more clearly than ever why it's crucial for parents to establish and maintain clearly defined boundaries, protective fences if you will, for their children. We'll talk about these in the next chapters.

CHAPTER NINE

Establishing Loving Boundaries: Part 1

Who would have thought that ignoring a boundary would nearly lead to death? Certainly not my friend Jim and I (Gary). But that's exactly what happened. As young boys growing up in the state of Washington, Jim and I heard over and over from his mother, "Don't go near that area around Boulder Flats." Boulder Flats had been the bed of a local river until a major flood had changed its course. Now it was several acres of various sized river rocks that had been fenced in by the park service.

Well, you know how curious boys can be. Not only was I curious, but coming from a home where there were no boundaries, I felt that fences were something to disrupt my life, not protect it.

It was a beautiful late summer morning, and Jim and I had been hiking through the nearby woods. Lunch time was right around the corner, so we (or maybe I'd better say *I*) decided we should take a short cut home—right through Boulder Flats. After all, if we skipped across the rocks, we could cut a half-hour off our walk back into town and be at the bridge that crossed the river in no time. From there, we'd be home for lunch before you knew it. For ten-year-old boys, hunger can make a short cut sound mighty tempting!

The barbed wire fence was old and feeling the effects of time, and who reads those Keep Out signs anyway? Pulling apart the barbed wire in one particularly shaky section, I let Jim in, and then he held the wires so I could get through.

We scrambled out onto the rocks and started jumping across them. We were making great time and doing just fine. At least that's what we thought. It wasn't until we were in the middle of the riverbed that we realized we were in trouble. Serious trouble.

When we jumped onto a big rock halfway across the dry stream, all around us the quiet morning air was suddenly shattered by the hissing and piercing sounds of rattlesnakes. As we held on to each other, we could see that we had landed right in the middle of a snake pit. Squirming in and out of the smaller rocks around us were dozens of rattlesnakes. Small snakes and large snakes as thick as your fist lay coiled or moved around and under the rocks. For what seemed like hours, we clung to that rock yelling for help at the top of our lungs and trying not to lose our footing.

The day went by, and no help came. As the afternoon sun dipped lower toward the hills, we decided that if we were ever to get free of the snakes, we had no choice but to try to continue across the river bottom.

Near the rock where we stood were several pieces of driftwood, relics of a time when water ran freely down this once mighty river. But there would be no chance of water washing away the snakes now, nor of our getting help from anyone who might have happened along. We were over a mile from the nearest house, and besides, everybody knew to avoid Boulder Flats! Picking up two long pieces of driftwood, we began the terrible journey across the riverbed.

There's no way I can convey to you the horror of the next hour and what it was like to gather up all our courage and jump from one large rock to another, knowing that if we slipped and fell to the ground, snakes would strike us before we could get back up to safety. At times, we used our driftwood sticks to beat at the rattlers from our perches. At one point, we used the sticks to lift up baby rattlesnakes and throw them out of the way.

Crying, praying, hoping, losing hope, we made our way across the riverbed. Finally, after an hour and a lifetime, we jumped from the last rock down onto the sand and ran up the river bank to safety.

Days later, when we had regained the emotional strength to think clearly about what had happened that horrible afternoon, we could remember over twenty snakes we had killed and dozens of others we had struck at with our sticks or tossed out of the way. We told our story to the park service, so a number of men and a small bulldozer went to Boulder Flats. They said they captured or killed over three hundred snakes—some of them trophy length!

Ignoring a boundary had nearly cost us our lives. Jim and I had been more than fortunate. The Lord had protected us from certain death had we fallen amidst all the snakes. The lessons I learned that terrible afternoon have taught me something very important about healthy families, particularly about parents who don't realize what's at stake with their children.

Every day, we see parents who fail to put up adequate boundaries for their children, and as a result their sons and daughters walk right into their own Boulder Flats. Although theirs may not contain rattlesnakes, these children face emotional and spiritual problems that are just as deadly because they received little supervision or were allowed to ignore warning signs, or their parents never took the time to put up the signs in the first place.

How can you put up healthy boundaries for your children that can protect them from the many "Boulder Flats" experiences of life? Why *should* you provide boundaries for your children? What kinds of boundaries are most important? In the pages that follow, let's learn more about how healthy boundaries build children's sense of worth and how you can best set up protective fences for them.

PROVIDING HEALTHY BOUNDARIES FOR CHILDREN

When we write about family boundaries, we're referring to protective "fences" put around a child for his security, support, and accountability. They give a child a sense of these things as he clearly sees limits on acceptable and unacceptable behavior. They also provide much-needed accountability when it comes to opening his life to positive people and experiences while closing the door to negative ones.

There was a time when parents didn't need to be reminded to provide boundaries for their children, but our permissive society seems to have changed all that. While we most certainly live in an age of grace, *tolerance* in many homes has become another word for *license*.

Unfortunately, the children in those "limit-less" homes are suffering the most. Here are just a few examples of situations we've seen personally or have read about this past year where parents have failed to provide healthy boundaries (protective fences) for their children.

- *Wanting to be liked and considered "in" by their teen-ager's friends, the parents provided an open bar at their daughter's party. Later that night, beyond the legal level of intoxication, a boy from the party sneaks out his parents' car, and he and another friend are killed in an automobile accident.*
- *A religion teacher at a major southwestern university says in an ethics class, "When my daughter turned sixteen, I put her on the pill. High school is a time for experimenting, and I wanted her to feel free to experiment."*
- *A nine-year-old is left alone to baby-sit his two younger sisters. A fire breaks out in the home, and all three children are killed while the mother is at her bowling league.*
- *A father sits in our office, crying because he has just found out his sixteen-year-old daughter is on drugs and pregnant from an immoral relationship with a twenty-six-year-old divorced man. He tells us, "We didn't want her to date him, but what could we say?"*
- *Even though they know their neighbor is actively involved in a popular cult that stresses "family values," they let those neighbors take their children*

to their church, where the kids become "enlightened."
Now the children will have nothing to do with their
parents' church or with them—unless they, too, join
this cult.

Extreme examples? Perhaps. But every day we see children who are growing up outside protective boundaries and who are left alone to steer their lives on an unmarked road. We realize that some parents provide too many and too firm boundaries for their children, and we'll address them later. However, we have found that parents who provide virtually no boundaries prevail. By their failure to have the courage and genuine love to set up and enforce clear boundaries, they can dishonor children and greatly lower their sense of significance and security.

Because of this, before we look specifically at the kinds of boundaries to set up, let's look at two reasons in this chapter (and two additional reasons in the next) why protective fences around children's behavior are essential, not optional.

THE IMPORTANCE OF PROVIDING PROTECTIVE BOUNDARIES

Boundaries Help Children Know They Are Loved.

One major way God communicates to His children that they are loved is by setting up a protective boundary around them and *disciplining* them if they go outside the fence of His Word.

"My son, do not despise the chastening [discipline]
of the LORD. . . . For whom the LORD loves He chas-
tens. [He chases them back inside His fence.]"
God deals with you as with sons; for what son is
there whom a father does not chasten? But if you are
without chastening . . . you are illegitimate and not
sons (Hebrews 12:5–8).

In our study of the Scriptures, we can't find a single example of God's loving someone where He didn't discipline him when he walked outside the perimeter of His Word. God loved Adam and Eve and provided a perfect environment for them to live in. Yet when they moved outside God's boundaries in the Garden, they were disciplined.[1]

Abraham lied, and he was disciplined.[2] Sarah laughed at the wrong time, and she was disciplined.[3] Moses may have faced up to the greatest leader of his day and taken God's people right out from under the Pharaoh's nose, but he was disciplined when he moved outside of God's limits and struck the rock twice.[4]

We could add Samson, Saul, David, Solomon, Peter, and others whom we will one day see in heaven, people who experienced God's love and, because they were loved, were disciplined when they erred. It doesn't mean that none of these saints were forgiven. What it does mean is that there were boundaries set up for their actions.

The word *discipline* comes from the Aramaic root "to bind."[5] When we discipline someone, we rope or bind him in. The New Testament word carries a word picture as well. It was used of young athletes who were taught to compete in a game by "having to stay within the lines."[6]

Do we mean to say that people who are "bound" and are made to "stay within the lines" feel loved? Before you toss aside this book, give us a minute to explain. Limits or boundaries do indeed give a person a feeling of security and safety. A study of young children showed just that.[7]

Security Means Staying Behind Protective Fences. Two groups of early grade-school children were studied during recess at several different schools over a long period of time. The schools had the same playground equipment, the same length of time for the children to play, and the same ratio of teachers to students. What was different between the two groups? One group was playing in a fenced playground, while the other group's playground had no fence and lay in a large, open field.

When the study was over, which group showed more cooperative play, had fewer playground fights, and exhibited lower levels of anxiety? Which group used more space on the playground and had better attitudes toward school work following recess? The kids who played in the wide open spaces? Wrong. The children with the boundaries of a fence were far and away happier and better adjusted. Why?

Children with clear boundaries feel a security that other children do not. Many of the youngsters in the fenced-in playground would run right up to and along the fence, feeling free to test their limits but also feeling secure behind them. The children in the group with nothing but open space stayed inside a smaller area on their playground than the children with the fenced-in boundaries.

Living without clear, protective boundaries can cause real problems. That is part of the reason God has given us such clear boundaries in His Word.

A Necessary Element of Genuine Love: Discipline. If we are God's children and we step outside the protective fences He sets up, we're asking to be disciplined. We all need discipline, the encouragement to get back inside His protective fences, if we want to grow and mature. Being disciplined is a clear demonstration that God loves us.

Genuine love (agape love) means committing ourselves willfully and sacrificially to another's best interests.[8] Christ demonstrated this when He died for us on the cross. Even in that act, God's love was poured out in discipline on His only Son, as Christ bore our sins that resulted from our willfully stepping outside the fence of His Word.

If love and discipline are inseparable, two things follow: first, *genuine love involves self-discipline.* If we have no boundaries for our actions and attitudes (like worry, anger, tone of voice, following through on promises, etc.), no guidelines to direct us or ropes to bind us to what is right, we have no healthy, balanced love to pass on to our children.

Second, *if we genuinely love and want the best for our children, we will discipline them.* From an early age, most children seem to understand that love and discipline can and do go together. Children may never ask for a spanking, but frequently, children who break a rule or do something wrong feel the need to be disciplined. They need to know that there are limits that are enforced and that aren't going to change on an hourly basis.

My (Gary's) little niece was playing one time with a crystal dish that normally sat on the living room table. Tammie knew the dish was off limits. Nonetheless, when she held it up to the light to get a prism effect and see all the pretty colors of refracted light, she accidentally dropped the dish, and it smashed into little pieces.

Tammie's mother was in the other end of the house in the kitchen, getting dinner ready. When she looked up, in came Tammie with her head hanging low and dragging her daddy's special drafting ruler (the family "Board of Education"). "Mommy, you're going to have to spank me," she said. And she went on to explain the whole story to her mother.

"You're right, Tammie," her mother said. "You know we've talked to you about not handling that dish and what would happen if you broke it." Then she gave her a swat on the bottom with the ruler. What her mother didn't know was that Tammie had a pencil in the back pocket of her jeans. When she got the swat, the ruler broke.

The spanking over, her mother hugged her and told her she loved her. Feeling better because she had been loved and disciplined, Tammie went back to playing around the house.

Lest you think Tammie is ready for sainthood, her mother told her she needed to tell her father about the spanking when he got home from work. When he walked in the door, do you know what her first words were? "Daddy, Daddy, Mommy broke your ruler!"

Children might not like discipline, but it tells them that they are valuable enough to have somebody set limits for them. This was something Karl never felt.

Withhold Boundaries and We Withhold Genuine Love. Karl was one of the saddest cases we've seen in counseling. It wasn't that he was treated that badly in his home. It's just that he was treated indifferently. It was almost as if he were an insignificant vapor not worth bothering about.

Karl grew up in a "blended" family. When Karl's mother

died, his father married a woman with three other children fairly close to Karl's age. Karl's stepmother wasn't intentionally cruel to him, but she did do something that was very unloving. She never disciplined him or set boundaries for him.

Her children had to turn off the television set at night to study, but Karl could stay up until midnight if he wanted. Let one of her children fail a test or get a bad conduct report from a class, and the thunder clouds would fill the air. If something similar happened to Karl, however, not a cloud would appear. It wasn't that this mother was leaving all of Karl's discipline to his father. When push came to shove, in comparison to "her children," she simply didn't think he was worth taking the time to correct. Her natural children or even her television shows were more important than her stepson.

Karl's stepmother provided hot meals and material things for him, but she didn't give him the most important thing he needed, a feeling of being genuinely loved and highly valued. Even though she occasionally told him she loved him, he never for a minute believed it. How could he? Every day he saw loving limits placed on his stepbrothers and stepsister and only a paper-thin permissiveness applied to him. Karl wanted to feel like a son. But all he got out of his stepmother's actions was a feeling that he was an illegitimate, unwanted child. We're convinced that many moms and dads simply don't realize that boundaries communicate such high value to their children, or that the lack of limits communicates such low value.

Boundaries Protect Children from Jumping Too Far Ahead.

I (Gary) can remember another time when I learned something boundaries could do for me. They could protect me from jumping too far ahead of myself.

Nearby the home where I grew up was a huge lumberyard where my father once worked. One day I went with him to the mill to watch the sawing machinery in action and to see all the timber being prepared for cutting.

I can remember my father's saying to me before he went in to talk to the shop foreman, "Gary, you can wander around all you like until I get back, but stay out of the sawdust pit. When I get through with the foreman, I'll show you that myself." Of course, as soon as he disappeared, the sawdust pit was the very first place I headed.

Stretched out before me was a beautiful sight. Like freshly fallen, unspoiled snow, a layer of sawdust lay over the top of a pit some twenty yards wide and over fifty yards long. Talk about a temptation! I took one quick look around to make sure my father wasn't in sight and then set off in my brand-new canvas tennis shoes to put my footprints across the length of that pit.

I was having the time of my life plowing up the sawdust until I had run about a third of the way across the pit. All of a sudden I realized my feet were burning! What I didn't know before I jumped into the sawdust was that I was running on top of a burning pit. Sawdust covered the top four inches, but beneath was a smoldering, red-hot fire! Turning around as fast as I could, I broke the land speed record getting back to safety. But even so, my new tennis shoes were ruined, and my feet were badly burned. I had jumped ahead of my father's promise, and my blistered feet reminded me of that fact.

Providing boundaries can keep a child from running too far ahead in life and burning himself in the process. In a very real sense, providing boundaries today can secure a child's tomorrow. Take the area of dating, for example.

It's becoming almost old-fashioned for parents to provide healthy boundaries for the kind of person a child can date and the time to come home from that date. Old-fashioned or not, however, you can protect a child's future. In addition, when you talk to your children about God's view of sexual standards in dating, and when you give them the added help of setting boundaries in this area, you can guide them away from the smoldering consequences of jumping ahead of God's plan for sexual intimacy.

Sexual intimacy outside of marriage is much like that sawdust pit. It may look safe and inviting. Yet the further someone goes, the greater the chances of getting badly burned. As a child, I had no idea what I was running into. All I knew was that it looked like something exciting to do. Even though something may look very exciting and appealing to your children, one of the privileges you have as a loving leader in your home is to point out the pain they cannot see that may lie right under the surface.

We once heard a definition of sin that went this way: "Sin is doing the right thing at the wrong time." That's not too bad a definition. When our Lord was tempted in the wilderness, there was nothing wrong with His turning stones into loaves of bread. After all, only a few weeks later He took a few loaves and fishes and fed several thousand people. It wasn't even wrong for Him to throw Himself down from the temple and let His angels catch Him. After all, they exist to be at His service (Hebrews 1:14) and certainly would have caught Him if He called.

What was wrong in each temptation was the timing. For Christ to do the right thing outside the boundary of God's perfect time would have been sin. Even today, many believers can be deceived into taking a good thing and choosing to do it at the wrong time. There is nothing wrong with sexual intimacy, for example, yet outside of God's right timing in marriage, it can lead to years of hurt in exchange for only a few moments of pleasure (Proverb 6:20ff.).

Perhaps your child wants to rush ahead and be sixteen years old when he or she is really eight. Don't lose hope. Wise parents make, communicate, and *stick by* healthy boundaries that can save their children many fiery hurts associated with emotional sawdust pits.

As we've been reminded in this chapter, setting up protective fences helps a child feel secure and loved and also provides a way to protect him from running too far ahead of what's right. In the next chapter we'll look at two additional by-products of setting healthy boundaries: adding productive days to our children's lives and helping them understand that there are biblical absolutes in an ever-changing world.

CHAPTER TEN

Establishing Loving Boundaries: Part 2

By this point in the book, we're sure that many of you are wondering how I (Gary) ever made it through my childhood days alive. But, something else I experienced as a child taught me another benefit of stable, protective boundaries. If I had learned this lesson earlier, it could have saved me from having the worst nightmare I'd ever experienced.

As a young boy, I (Gary) had been fishing on a beautiful lake in the Northwest. It was foresting country, and at many places along the lake, logs lay alongside each other in the water where they would soon be floated down to the mill. At one place on the lake, a good distance from where I stood, logs had been tied together to make a walking path out to a small island. From everything I'd heard from the old-timers around the lake, it was the perfect place to fish.

As I began the long walk toward the manmade bridge, I started thinking about the "natural" bridge right in front of me. Those logs stretched right out to the island, and they were so many and so thick that it would be no trick at all to get right to that great fishing spot and save the walk to the manmade bridge! Why waste time walking all the way to where the logs were tied together? I had a walkway right in front of me.

Chuckling to myself over the brilliance of my discovery, I ran on top of the logs out toward the island. Everything went well at first. The logs were so thick that there was very little give in them. Unfortunately, what I couldn't tell from the shore was that the logs got increasingly smaller in diameter as I got closer to the island. When I began, I could step on a log, and it would go down only a few inches. As the logs got smaller with each step I took, I sank lower and lower into the water until that last fateful step.

Even though the logs were still thickly bunched together, they had become so skinny that when I put my foot down, it slid right between the wet logs and suddenly I was underwater with a major problem. My fall had forced the logs apart momentarily, but just as quickly they moved right back together. As I fought my way up for air, the logs had formed a wooden roof above me that I didn't have the strength to pull apart.

Thrashing around underwater, desperately looking for the smallest opening, I found a crack between two logs and forced my arm and head out of the water, gasping for breath. As I crawled out on top of the logs, which barely held me afloat, I was wet, frightened, angry, exhausted, and embarrassed. I had also lost all my fishing gear—and nearly my life. What had looked like a tremendous short cut had turned into a long, life-threatening ordeal! For weeks I woke up in the middle of the night, fighting my way out of the covers as I dreamed I wasn't able to find a way through the logs to the surface.

Something I've seen many times since that experience is that cutting corners is often a good way to add time and energy to any project. In fact, another "Smalley-Trent Axiom of Life" is "It almost always takes twice as long to get out of something as it did to get into it!"

What does all this have to do with building self-worth and honoring children? Parents who want to see their children's sense of value go up need to set boundaries for short cuts that can damage their lives. These include corners they can be tempted to cut to gain a friend, win a promotion, or get out of a spanking.

BOUNDARIES ADD PRODUCTIVE DAYS
TO CHILDREN'S LIVES

When you establish clear boundaries for short cuts your children are tempted to take, you add days of peace and productivity to their lives. How is this possible? Let's look at a common short cut many people take in life and see how much work and anxiety it can cause and how much joy it can rob. That short cut is lying.

While stumping along the political trail one year, Abraham Lincoln was asked by a reporter why he always made it a habit to tell the truth. "There is a very good reason why I strive to tell the truth," Lincoln replied. "It means I don't have as much to remember!"[1]

Have you ever lied to someone or a group of people and had a hard time keeping your story straight? One problem with lying is that it gives you so little rest! It may have saved you from a spanking, kept you from losing face, or gained you favor in someone's eyes, but the lack of peace it leaves in your life can eventually turn on you.

The Bible puts it this way: "A false witness will not go unpunished,/And he who speaks lies will not escape."[2] Lying is like having a severely twisted ankle. As long as you walk slowly and carefully, you can often hide your lack of support. However, there's always the fear that you'll twist a conversation too far or put too much pressure on your alibi and fall flat on your face.

Establishing boundaries for lying honors your children and shows them you are serious about loving them. Why? Because it helps them experience the freedom of telling the truth and keeps them within protective fences.

A Short Cut to Disaster

If you let little white lies go, your children can begin the descent into darkness. As their lies mount, they can experience the trauma of lying awake at night, knowing in the back of their minds that this may be the day their lies are discovered.

Duke Tully bore such a burden. For over twenty years,

Duke was the editor of the largest newspaper in a major Sun Belt city. To newspaper opponents or to anyone else in the state who dared attack him or the paper, the Duke was as fierce a foe as John Wayne ever hoped to be. He was almost as tough on his friends and coworkers.

But hey, this was the Duke, a decorated combat pilot who flew missions in World War II, Korea, and Vietnam. No wonder he was so hard-nosed. One look at the combat pictures and decorations on the walls in his office would tell you why.

Just stand around him at those Veteran's Day functions, look at the decorations on his uniform, and listen to him swap war stories with the best of them. You could take it to the bank, old Duke was as much at home with men he knew like Joe Foss, World War II flying ace and Medal of Honor winner, as he was with any of his editors on the paper.

The only problem was that Duke Tully was never in the service. He never served during any war, never flew a combat mission.

It all began as a simple little lie about being in the service so that he could impress some people, but he kept adding embellishments to the story. It may have started out as flying combat missions in World War II, but then there was also Korea. And, oh yes, did we mention Vietnam?

Eventually, to back up his story and protect himself from questioning eyes, Duke had to purchase a uniform and get pictures made of himself beside various planes. And always, always, there had to be that gnawing feeling inside his stomach as he lay awake at night trying to remember what he said, when he had said it, and to whom.

Can you imagine the nights this man must have had, knowing that ultimately liars can't escape from all their words? Would you want *your* child to go through the humiliation and public ridicule this man has faced since the true facts of his story came out? Not indicating boundaries for your own words or your children's speech could lead you to a similar fate sooner than you think.

Lying isn't the only short cut children are tempted to take. A similar thing happens with other self-control issues such as studying. We can't tell you how many young men and women we've known who never had a protective fence around weeknights in grade school and high school when they had homework due. Then in their first year of college, the students awoke to a shattering reality when they began to flunk out of school. Because they never had a boundary set for their school evenings as they were growing up, they didn't know the first thing about how to study or how to set study times, and their grades and failing slips reflected it.

When you establish legitimate, healthy boundaries for areas of hurt into which your children can stray, you honor them by saving them twice the work and time of trying to get themselves out of something you should have put a protective fence around in the first place.

BOUNDARIES HELP CHILDREN UNDERSTAND THAT THERE ARE ABSOLUTES

At the time we're writing this book, a popular television commercial pictures a large bull walking freely in a number of different locations. On an ocean beach, in the middle of a city, out in the wheat fields of the Midwest—like the five-hundred-pound canary, it goes anywhere it wants. And all the time, in the background a chorus sings "We know no boundaries." This commercial is supposed to demonstrate to investors what financial freedom is all about.

Unfortunately, for families who know no boundaries, the lack of limits demonstrates to children the absence of biblical absolutes. What do we mean by an "absence of absolutes"?

People without an absolute standard are ultimately left without a lasting value system. What is "right" today almost certainly won't be "right" in the future. (Would any of us alive in 1957 have imagined that "gay rights" activists would control entire political structures in certain cities as they do today?) Erwin Lutzer, in his excellent little book *The Necessity of Ethical Absolutes*,[3] points out that as a result of the uncertainty that goes along with situational ethics and our society's ever-changing values, people lose the ability to say no. Inadequate absolutes soon lead a person to inadequate morals.

Our trying to base absolutes on culture, situational ethics, or emotions is like a spider trying to build a web on the hands of a clock. Each tick of the clock pulls at the inadequate structure that's been set up hurriedly and will soon tear it apart, leaving the spider forever mending holes and always shifting positions.

Children who grow up in homes without consistent boundaries fall prey to the same problems a society faces when it leaves the protective fence provided by God's absolute, authoritative Word: inadequate identity and decisions based on feelings or glands, not what's lasting or right. Let's allow Todd's story to illustrate how such a home can undermine a child's self-worth and destroy his future.

Cut Adrift from an Absolute Anchor

Todd's parents were so concerned about not disciplining him for the wrong things that they rarely disciplined him at all. They loved to brag at parties that they had "never laid a hand" on their son to correct him. After all, they grew up in a permissive society and an even more permissive church. As far as his liberated parents were concerned, there were no commandments in Scripture for "our age," rather, just "meaningful suggestions." As a result, clear boundaries for questionable practices were placed in the file marked "nonexistent."

Because Todd grew up knowing no boundaries, nothing anyone said to correct or instruct him ever carried much weight. Why should it? For Todd, if even God's Word was up for grabs, anything a teacher or coach or boss had to say to him carried as much weight as the air used to convey the words

Children learn the basis of right and wrong in their homes. And if nothing was wrong, Todd assumed that meant that anything he felt like doing must be right. This included hitting, swearing, lying, and stealing from his friends.

Growing up without boundaries can become addictive. Like a horse that hasn't been bridled and ridden in months and then has a bit forced into its mouth and a saddle slapped on its back, a child who runs into the inescapable boundaries of life when he or she has rarely experienced them before will rebel.

Todd fought and kicked against anything and anyone who tried to put a protective fence around his actions. What made the story even sadder was that Todd's parents stood back and watched all this happening to him, never once having the courage or the genuine love to step in and help him or to admit they were a part of the problem.

With all the anger and restlessness that had developed in Todd's life, and with almost no controls on that anger from his parents, Todd became a textbook liar and a junior-grade criminal (sociopath). He would lie to and defy his parents to their faces, and he was allowed to dishonor them at every step. Every time he got away with dishonoring Mom and Dad by his actions and attitudes, he grew to believe he shouldn't suffer any negative consequences for dishonoring others. After all, anything goes.

As we mentioned earlier, when we dishonor our parents, we lower our own value because we're so much like them. Feeling out of control and insecure, Todd acted out how much he disliked himself. With no boundaries to corral his negative feelings and his mounting anger, his frustrations began to explode whenever he was at school or around his rapidly diminishing group of friends.

When his teacher tried to do something about his aggressive behavior and unwillingness to do his homework, she was met with back talk, anger, and glaring eyes. When his Little League coach benched him for swearing and throwing his bat when he struck out, he quit the team. A few years later, when his boss at the grocery store asked him to stay and work an extra hour, Todd refused and lost his job.

And what about God? What *about* Him? The last person Todd wanted anything to do with was Someone who calls on people to give up their lives and live His way. Besides, from what his parents had taught him, he couldn't believe God's words anyway.

Todd was angry with everyone except his parents, he thought. They never got in his way like all those other people. What he didn't realize was that the anger he spewed out on others stemmed from the original frustrations he felt toward Mom and Dad. He liked the way they let him "do his thing" by putting lewd posters in his room and smoking dope in the house, but he wasn't discerning enough to know how much they were hurting him by doing so. He couldn't see it at the time, but his parents were doing him incredible harm by ignoring biblical absolutes.

Even when they were confronted with this truth months later, his parents refused to acknowledge their part in his anger or their weakness in being unwilling to confront him. If only once they had stood up to him, perhaps they could have begun to reverse a terrible downward slide.

Why does the lack of boundaries cause such angry behavior in children? In some ways, it's very much like what happens to men during war.

Casualties Too Close to Home

High levels of frustration and anger are a common denominator for men who have been in combat, even long after the battles are over. In talking with a number of Vietnam veterans, one researcher noted that the lack of safe boundaries overseas or at home lay at the heart of many men's complaints.[4]

War produces casualties of many types, and among them are soldiers who carry around tremendous anger because of living in a place without safe boundaries. Homes without the safe boundaries set up by loving parents produce casualties of their own—children like Todd.

Go without getting a healthy night's rest for a week, and watch how irritable and easily frustrated you become. Go without boundaries for years, and watch how deep and uncontrollable your anger becomes.

Like the children on the playground without a fence, Todd learned through his unnamed anxieties never to drop his guard. As a result of constantly feeling insecure and unprotected by his parents, Todd's deep-rooted anger brought him to the place where he couldn't care less what happened to himself or others. And because he demanded too much too soon and felt he was beyond any "absolute" rules, he was arrested at age sixteen—for selling drugs to two nine-year-olds.

In a world where everything is relative, Todd and many children like him are handed a road map with no north and south markings and left to wander into terrible places of self-destruction without a compass with a "true" north. They need clear boundaries that are marked off by biblical absolutes.

Before we go on to talk about what kinds of boundaries are best and how to set them up, we need to issue one vital caution. Most children have a natural mind-set that can make your setting and sticking with boundaries very difficult.

ANYTHING BUT A WARM RESPONSE

According to the Scriptures, the wise man loves you when you correct him, and he'll meet you with thanks and appreciation. What about those who aren't so wise, however? Unfortunately, you can't expect such a warm response from the unwise. A fool's reaction to correction is anger, and sometimes active hostility (Proverbs 9:7–8).

What does this have to do with children and establishing boundaries for them? There is another verse that says, "Foolishness is bound up in the heart of a child" (Proverb 22:15). That verse helps you get the whole picture. By nature, children (like adults) have to grow into maturity and wisdom. It isn't a "given"; it's earned by learning the skill of living God's way.

When you honor your children by providing loving boundaries for them, in the long run they'll become more enjoyable for you and for others to live with. However, there will probably be times when they'll become angry with you for suggesting legitimate restrictions for them.

When a child builds up all his fury and declares that he's going to attend that certain concert, watch that show, stay up until 4:30 A.M. on a school night, or spend the night with the guys in their fort, many parents fail to follow through on maintaining boundaries, even those that will protect a child from major hurts. The unfortunate thing is that the lower a parent's self-worth and personal value, the more insecure he'll be and the more difficulty he may have in dealing with his child's anger at legitimate restrictions. Sometimes we honor someone by disciplining him, yet many insecure parents have great difficulty with this kind of tough love.

An Effective Barrier to Setting Up Protective Boundaries

Every parent loses his heart to that little boy or girl who looks up at him with a smile from the crib, sits in his lap, or flashes him that award-winning grin. However, when a person has never been loved or felt valuable himself, his child's love can mean more than normal parental attachment. It can also make up for years of past hurts.

When a child is angry with you, particularly when you establish boundaries for his actions, he often wants to have nothing to do with you for a short period of time. For an insecure parent, having to face a child's anger toward him, even for a few hours, can be too burning a pain to take. Cut off from the love he's received from that child, he's reminded too much of the years he's spent feeling alone and unwanted. Even in a home in which one parent tries to be more firm with the child to make up for the other parent who is not, watch how the insecure parent sabotages any attempt to discipline that "poor little lamb"—the same child who just broke the neighbor's chair by jumping up and down on it.

Watching their children relax and even smile when they give in to them can be a tremendous relief to some parents. It's almost as if they go underwater when their children become angry with them and they're finally able to come up for air! Children quickly learn how dependent their parents can become on their good graces, and they can hold their parents hostage by withholding their love when they want to avoid a rule.

Children, even very young children, can pound on boundaries with incredible force to see if the limits are real. But with some parents, like Jericho of old, all their children have to do is march around them seven times with their arms crossed and "shout with a great shout" (Joshua 6:5), and the parents' walls come tumbling down.

When children beat down their parents' boundaries, they learn that they are the ones who set the limits in the home, and the injustice and the illogic of that can cause havoc for both parents and children.

Times of Testing in Single-Parent Homes

Single parents in particular typically go through a tremendous time of testing, especially if it's the dad who has moved out. For many children, Dad's "no" may be more frightening and harder to get around than Mom's, and Mom's natural sensitivity and relational skill make her vulnerable to attacks on the boundaries she sets up.

So single moms, expect to have your boundaries tested. When one parent leaves, a great amount of the children's security leaves, too, no matter how bad your "ex" may have been. Insecure children will often push against protective fences to make sure they really exist. Your children may try to make you think that you've become an unloving troll overnight in keeping them inside protective fences, but the clouds will begin to pass once they feel secure in your boundaries. If you give in to their testing demands, you'll have any number of days to regret your decision.

It's not nice to have someone "hate" you for a few hours or even for a few days, and it's tempting to give in. But one way you honor and eventually lead your children to wisdom is by holding fast to what's right instead of caving in because of their frowns. I (John) saw this illuminated in the loving actions of my aunt.

LOOKING BACK ON LOVING BOUNDARIES

During my seventh-grade year, my mother had a long convalescence after several major surgeries. Because of all the help we had with our extended family back in Indiana, she spent her time recuperating in the Midwest while my aunt came out to Arizona to keep watch over us three boys.

Aunt Dovie is small in stature, and when we had been with her at family gatherings, she had always seemed as gentle as a lamb. What we didn't know was that she was made of pure steel when it came to setting and keeping loving boundaries. Her strength didn't come overnight. It came from raising children of her own and being a model servant to the rest of the family for decades. For over seventy years now, her personal resources and faith in God have made her the person we all turn to in our family when we're in need of help.

Although we wouldn't admit it, we boys needed help. With our mother gone away to recuperate, we felt like the class that's just found out they're going to have a substitute! As a single parent, my mother did a tremendous job of making us toe the line. Send us little, gentle Aunt Dovie, and we were overjoyed. It would be wall-to-wall parties and staying up all night! But then we began to find out that her gentle spirit didn't mean she would give in on what was best for us and right in God's sight.

I'll be honest with you. There were times when she disciplined me and I became incredibly angry with her. (For instance, there was the time I sneaked out my window late one night to meet with a group of low-lifes who had dropped out of school, and I forgot to put the screen back on the window. "The screen? Oh, well, uh, you see, Aunt Dovie, the wind must have blown it off!")

My aunt never yelled at me. She didn't have to. Holding the screen in her hand and waiting for my answer, she only had to look at me with those steady eyes and uncompromising words that asked for the truth, and I felt burning conviction inside. Yet like many foolish adolescents (and adults), I felt only anger when she corrected me, not the conviction of the wise.

Even as a seventh-grader, I was taller than Aunt Dovie by several inches. I can remember looking down on her as she gently talked to me about being truthful and the importance of having positive friends. No matter how softly she spoke, her words would pound inside my head like a screaming lecture, and I would walk away when she was finished and slam the door behind me.

"The nerve of this woman," I would say to myself or shout out loud to the air. "Nobody died and left her queen! Who does she think she is, anyway, all five feet of her, trying to stop me from ruining my life?"

"Who does she think she is. . . ." Over the years, as I've looked back at that crucial time in my early adolescent years, I know who she was: an angel from heaven. Aunt Dovie cared enough to stand in the gap between a foolish adolescent boy who was reaching out to the wrong side and the evil that would have loved to draw him in. She cared enough to stand up to my anger, sarcasm, and disrespect for her for well over a year and never back down or stop loving me.

I know for a fact that I wouldn't be the man I am today if my Aunt Dovie hadn't loved me when I was so hard to love. Time and again my childhood foolishness came to the surface, and I fought with her. But her courage and her commitment to what was right and what would honor God and me pulled both of us through until my mother got back on her feet.

Deep down inside, even in the midst of my rebellion, I wanted someone to love me enough to correct me. It wasn't until several years later, however, that I had enough wisdom to understand how much she had loved me and to thank her for it. Today, years older and a little wiser, if I were to begin a list of people who have truly loved me over the years, I'd put Aunt Dovie and a few others like her near the top of the list.

We've looked at four reasons we should provide protective boundaries and one caution that could sidetrack us from doing so if our own self-worth is low. Now we're ready to focus on the kinds of boundaries that work best and how we can set them up.

CHAPTER ELEVEN

Establishing Loving Boundaries: Part 3

Earl and Judy had finally built their dream house away from the sprawling city, the never-ending traffic, and the increasing pollution. It was nestled at the base of a mountain some thirty-five miles north of Phoenix, and the unspoiled southwestern desert came right up to their doorstep.

The desert has its own beauty: numerous shades of brown laced with the khaki green of native trees and cacti, rocks of volcanic black and milk-white quartz, lavender sunrises, and golden, sun-splashed sunsets. But the desert also has its own danger, something Earl and Judy never took seriously.

It had taken every available dollar the couple had—and more—to complete their home. Trying to cut costs, they decided one thing they could skimp on was the fence they wanted put around the back yard. Even though the few neighbors near them had concrete block or tall, chain-link fences around the area where children and pets would play, Earl and Judy decided that for the time being, a small wooden-rail fence would do just as well.

It was late in the afternoon on a beautiful spring day, and soon Earl would be driving down their gravel driveway after working in the city. Judy was at the sink, finishing her preparations for dinner, and the children had just come inside from playing in the back yard. That's when she heard their little dog, Muffin, barking hysterically near the side of the house.

Instantly, Judy looked up from the sink and out the window that gave her a clear view of the yard. What she saw was terrible. Four coyotes had jumped through the wooden fence and were attacking Muffin.

Before she could get the back door open, the battle was over. As she stepped outside, she saw the coyotes dragging the still form of the family pet under the fence. Crying and yelling, she could only watch as they disappeared into the desert. Through her tears, she was thankful that her two young children had not been in the back yard as well.

Because our children are more precious than our "Muffins," we continually urge parents to get involved and take seriously the need to set up positive, protective boundaries for children. We've encouraged you to put up protective fences against things and people that can rush in like coyotes and damage your children emotionally or physically, or sneak in and destroy their self-worth.

What types of fences do the best job of protecting children and of raising their value? Do children have any say in the boundaries that are set up? Can boundaries provide security but still allow freedom for positive development?

We can find some of the answers in the very hand that holds this book or the eyes that read it. The Lord has provided a picture of well-functioning boundaries right in the human body.

PUMPING IN GOOD AND PUSHING OUT BAD

Every inch of the body is made up of millions and millions of cells, each of which can teach us something about positive boundaries. Although this is obviously an oversimplified explanation,[1] let's zoom in and focus on just one cell.

Like every other cell in the body, the one we've selected has a boundary (cell membrane) around it. We could picture that boundary as a fence that runs all the way around it. All along this fence are a number of gates (actually, little pump mechanisms). Picture each gate with a little guard watching over it who is responsible for opening and closing the gate.

Some of these gates only open in, letting in good things the cell needs such as essential nutrients and antibodies to fight disease. Others only open out and are used for removing bad things that have somehow gotten inside the cell. These would include certain waste by-products of cell function and toxic substances that may have slipped in under the fence or gotten inside the cell through an unmanned or malfunctioning gate.

In a healthy cell, the little guards stay on duty day and night to carry out their specific functions. However, should disease or injury affect the cell, the fence around it can begin to deteriorate. When this happens, the little guards can be affected and fail to properly operate their gates. As a result, many gates that should be opening for needed nutrients stay closed, and other gates are left closed that should be opening to expel destructive elements that have accumulated. Ultimately, when a cell's protective fence breaks down, it signals the destruction of the cell.

As parents, we can learn about setting boundaries from looking at that cell. First, *the absence of boundaries almost ensures the presence of problems*. As we've observed in the last few chapters, a child can be much more easily carried away or infected with problems from peer pressure to petty thievery when there is no protective fence around him or her.

Second, *every fence we put around a child should have two different gates in it*. One is to let in positive words, experiences, and people, and the other is to remove or keep out as many bad experiences and agents as possible.

Isn't it interesting how God designed within each healthy cell both types of gates? Good things need to come in, but the expectation is that there will also be bad things that need to be removed. For parents, these two functions of "manning the gates" for children are just as important as setting up protective boundaries in the first place.

If you haven't asked yourself the question yet, consider it now: "How involved and faithful a guard am I in 'manning the gates' for my children?" The answer can determine much of how secure and stable is their future.

The book of Proverbs calls us to guard our spiritual lives by keeping out wrong and keeping diligent watch, for the good God will bring:

> *Blessed is the man who listens to me,*
> *Watching daily at my gates,*
> *Waiting at the posts of my doors.*
> *For whoever finds me finds life,*
> *And obtains favor from the LORD.*
> *(Proverbs 8:34–35)*

Parents who watch over the gates of their children's lives are also a blessing to their children. But now you may ask, "How many boundaries should I set up around my children, and how do I know what to let in or put out?"

We've discovered that the healthiest homes aren't necessarily those that have the most rigid or the greatest number of boundaries. Neither are they the ones that have so many gates left open that every experience is allowed to wash over their children unchecked.

Rather, the ones that cause the greatest growth in their children's self-worth are those that base their boundaries on four simple questions that help to keep a home in balance. These four questions are ones that each of us, young or old, is continually answering as we interact with others, and the results of our answers either raise or lower our self-worth.[2]

FOUR QUESTIONS THAT HELP SHAPE POSITIVE BOUNDARIES

Question #1: "Who Am I?"

Every parent needs to set up a protective fence around the question each child will eventually ask, "Who am I?" Nearly every week, we see the damage done to a child who left home not knowing the answer to this question.

Boys and girls (some of them now adults) who didn't grow

up inside the safety of loving parental and biblical boundaries often leave home without a positive sense of identity. As a result, their search to find an answer to this question often leads them to try damaging and devaluing solutions. Time after time, they find unfulfilling answers in alcoholism, immorality, workaholism, and broken relationships.

We need to know who we are if we're to stand on our own or relate successfully to others. Like individuals living in a house of mirrors, we'll be left to wander the halls gazing at distorted images of ourselves if we can't picture who we are. Talk to one person or group, and we're terrific. Talk to another, and we're rejected without a second thought. Gaining a realistic, positive sense of identity can unlock the door and release us from the prison of having each group we're in or every Hollywood personality on television determine our character, values, and self-worth.

One reason Jesus was able to face persecution, trial, and the peer pressure to set Himself up as Rome's king or set Himself down as a blasphemer was His knowledge of who He was (John 8:58; 16:5–13). Your children need to know their identity if they are to have the confidence to face their future and stand strong. One way you can guide them toward a positive understanding of themselves is to teach them who they are *not*.

Show Them the Danger of the Inflated Self. From the earliest times, we human beings have had the tendency to answer the question of self-identity by saying we're something we're not.[3] Let's illustrate this by looking at some examples of everyday people.

Several studies have found that people tend to accept more responsibility for their successes than their failures, for their good deeds than their bad.[4] If their team wins, it's because of their superior athletic skills or cheering; if they lose, it's because of the crummy officiating. When they know which is the highest mountain in North America when asked in a Trivial Pursuit game, it's their brilliance that comes up with the answer; when they fail at the next question, it's because "nobody" knows the capital of Tibet.

In the excellent article "The Inflated Self," David Myers

pointed out that one common manifestation of low self-worth is *inflated* self-worth.[5] He built a strong case that pride is every bit as big a problem as low self-worth, and we agree.

Pride can certainly cloud the issue of self-identity. It can mask a deep sense of low self-worth as an imperfect person fights to "claim" an exalted identity he really doesn't feel inside.

Pride has pushed people to set themselves up as God's equal to gain a fleeting feeling of power and a sense that their lives have meaning. No matter how high we jump, however, we can never escape our feet of clay that pull us back to the ground.

Thankfully, Christians have an advantage in answering the question "Who am I?" because they can openly admit they are fallen and in need of a Savior. They don't need to wait centuries to evolve into a higher moral form (have morals risen in the years since you were born?), nor do they need to pass themselves off as "little gods," as one popular cult teaches (never truly believing such a claim in their heart of hearts when they see sin and error deep inside).

We can answer the question "Who am I?" and help our children answer it by understanding our fallen nature and the liberating freedom of being able to throw ourselves on God's grace. Doing so frees us from having to play God and gives us the power and acceptance we're struggling to get. This freedom is found in who we are in God's eyes.

Teach Them Their Identity in Christ. By teaching your children who God says they are, you honor them and help them leave home with high worth. His Word says that His children are deeply loved,[6] highly treasured,[7] of great worth,[8] only a little lower than the angels,[9] secure in His love,[10] His own special people,[11] made in His image,[12] of more value than the birds of the air,[13] and so important that God gave up His only Son to reclaim them from darkness.[14]

Every day, by teaching God's Word to your children and living it out before them, by having them listen to Christian music and allowing them to be with His people at church and at socials, you can build in positive words and thoughts that give them a secure identity in Christ. We'll take an entire chapter to highlight this point later,[15] but when children know how God views them, that can be the greatest single factor in building up their self-worth.

Give Them a Name to Live Up to—and Protect That Name. Who they are in Christ and who they are not apart from Him are two important areas around which you can build protective fences. Children also need to know how highly you view them to truly answer the question "Who am I?" And a good place to begin is with their own names.

DRAWING STRENGTH FROM THEIR NAME: ONE WAY TO LET GOOD THINGS IN

Letting a child know why you named her what you did can be a tremendous encouragement to her, especially if that name has biblical or some other special significance behind it. For example, each of us has a daughter named Kari. In Greek, *Kari* means "love from a pure heart."

For Gary and Norma's daughter, who is now in college and a delight to her parents, being told the meaning of her name when she was young has given her extra encouragement throughout the years to develop a pure, loving heart. For John and Cindy's infant daughter (who by the way was named after Gary's daughter), the name represents her parents' prayer for her and their commitment to raise her in an environment that reflects the virtues of her name.

In the Scriptures, a person's name always had great significance.[16] That's why God took special care in giving people names or in changing them. For example, in Peter's case, being called the Rock was a vivid reminder of his commission, of all he could become, and of how others would depend on him following the Resurrection (Matthew 16:18).

In addition to the attachment it can build between parent and child, there's another significant thing about naming a person: very often, children live up to the names they are called. And in that light, may we ask you a difficult question? Aside from their given names, what "names" are your children growing up with? Are they anything like the one a man in the restaurant booth next to us had for his son?

"Stump. That's what we call him," the burly man in the cap told us. "Oh, his name's really Billy, but just look at that neck. Show them your neck, Billy. Can you see that? He doesn't even have a neck! That's why we call him Stump. Come on, Stump. Show them your neck. Ha! Ha! Ha!"

This father never saw the way his preschool son hung his little head, never noticed the look of defeat and hurt that registered on his wife's face. But then again, she had to live with her own special name: "Cupcake—because she looks like a cupcake! Ha! Ha! Ha!"

Derogatory names can brutalize a child (or adult) and blast away at his self-worth. Some children have heard such names so often that they grow up thinking their name is "Stupid," "Clumsy," "Pudgy," or "Four Eyes" instead of Matt, Lisa, James, or Jill. Leave a negative label on a child too long, even if it's only in fun, and it can leave him feeling as if two all-pro linebackers have just smashed into him at full speed.

However, the opposite is true as well. Helping a child see the value in the names you give and call him can build worth and self-esteem in his life. I (Gary) recently witnessed the positive effects of my son's finding out more about his namesake. At the time of this writing, Greg is eighteen years old and a freshman in college. One of his assignments was to research his family tree. He had old photos and letters from relatives that I didn't even know he had kept.

Buried deep in his closet was a letter I had written Greg when he was first learning to read. It was a letter talking about why we had given him his name and who we had named him after. The letter was actually a detailed account of Cardinal Hildebrand, the eleventh-century clergyman who later became Pope Gregory VII. Through a relative who is a diligent historian, I had discovered that we were related to this saint of old on my mother's side, her name being Emily Hildebrand. As I had read about this man's life while I was in seminary, many of his qualities and character traits had impressed me. He was more than a church leader; he had a personal, vibrant relationship with Christ.

As I looked over Greg's shoulder while he reviewed the letter, he looked up at me and said, "Dad, is this really our relative and the person I was named after?" From the way he asked the question and commented on what he had learned, I could tell he read with honor about his namesake.

Taking time to point out the special significance of your children's names and being sure the pet names or nicknames you give them are helpful and not hurtful can open the gate to good things and help them answer the question "Who am I?"

A second way you can help them answer the question is to put *outside* the fence those words, people, or attitudes that tell them they are anything less than what God says they are. Take Karen, for example.

GUARDING THEIR NAME:
PUTTING BAD THINGS OUT

The vast majority of elementary school teachers are dedicated, caring professionals who build up children's self-worth. In fact, for many children in first grade, their teacher is the one they love the most after their parents and the one who sets the tone for their future expectations of school. In Karen's case, however, the teacher didn't inspire love. Mrs. Williams was a harsh, insensitive woman who evoked fear in her students with her frequent, angry outbursts.

Karen's parents had seen her excited and enthusiastic in her kindergarten class, but now they saw their daughter doing poorly in first grade. It wasn't that the material being taught was too difficult. Having been in a special reading camp over the summer, Karen was far ahead of many children in her class in writing and learning to read. But Karen was complaining of being sick more than ever before and was wanting to miss school with every complaint.

After searching for what could be affecting her so badly, her parents discovered the source of the problem. Angry words had robbed her of a positive identity and feelings of self-worth.

Karen was hearing two messages in her little life. One message at home and at church was that she was deeply loved and special to God and her parents. The other message was the one she received from her schoolteacher, who felt she was a bother and a pain. Her teacher had a pet name for her: "Miss Busybody."

From Karen's first day in school, her teacher had decided to make her an example to the other students to let them all know "who was boss." Being a talkative little girl, Karen was visiting with a classmate when the school bell rang, commencing class. The moment the bell sounded, an eraser flew across the room, hitting Karen in the back of the head. The flying eraser was followed by a barrage of angry words designed to put the "fear of Mrs. Williams" in her and the rest of the children. Needless to say, it worked.

Karen was a very sensitive child. In the days and weeks that followed, she had more and more difficulty in handling Mrs. Williams's angry outbursts. Some of the children would try to stand up to her or simply ignore her, but Karen could do neither. Sometimes her teacher could just look at her with those angry eyes when she walked by her desk, and Karen would begin to cry. Then she would get a lecture for being a "spoiled brat" and too emotionally immature for first grade.

Whether it was not lining up properly after recess or not putting away the paints as she should, Karen found the person she looked to for encouragement and support slamming emotional doors in her face almost daily. "No wonder you haven't gotten your assignments done, Miss Busybody," Mrs. Williams would typically say. "You can talk, but you can't do the homework!"

Like many children, Karen was too embarrassed and too loyal to her teacher to talk with her parents about what was happening at school.[17] Attempts by her mother and father to find out what was wrong were unsuccessful. At the first parent-teacher meeting, Karen's parents made a special point to talk to her teacher about Karen's behavior, and they found Mrs. Williams to be very pleasant. They were assured it was simply "the adjustment of a new school" that was affecting their daughter, and they went away puzzled, thinking the problem must lie with Karen.

However, as problems continued to mount, Karen's mother approached a young teacher's aide in the class, and she admitted and explained how dreadfully Karen was being treated in class. After an emotional confrontation between the principal, Mrs. Williams, the teacher's aide, and Karen's parents, Karen was transferred to another class, where they saw an almost instant improvement in her attitude and school work. As a result of the investigation the principal started after this meeting, the next year Mrs. Williams was transferred to an administrative position in the district away from any direct involvement with children.

If Karen's parents hadn't been sensitive enough to check the gates and monitor the words and names others repeatedly spoke to her as well as their own, little Karen would have been left with a confusing answer to the question "Who am I?"

Unfortunately, there's something within all of us (our fallen nature) that tends to throw out the positives we hear and put on the negatives. That's why monitoring the messages coming into our children's lives from outside sources can be every bit as important as being mindful of the messages we put in.

As important as it is to provide a healthy boundary for the question of self-identity, it is equally important to put up a fence around a second question, "Whom do I want to please?" As we'll show in the next chapter, children who can answer this in a healthy way gain confidence and self-worth by leaps and bounds.

CHAPTER TWELVE

Establishing Loving Boundaries: Part 4

My (John's) grandfather taught me a tremendous lesson about how loving boundaries can honor a child and help him feel tremendously valuable. That's because he taught me the importance of answering correctly the next question that should shape the boundaries we set up.

Question #2: "Whom Do I Want to Please?"

When I was in third grade, I was part of a gang of neighborhood kids who constantly roamed the streets, alleys, orange groves, and desert areas near our homes on our bicycles. I knew my mother's rules: we could ride our bikes anywhere we wanted, but we had to be home before the streetlights came on. Unfortunately for my brothers and me, there was a streetlight directly in front of our house that didn't allow for any "fudge factor" in being home on time.

One afternoon, I knew it was about time to start heading home, but I decided to listen to one of my friends instead. He said, "Forget about going home now! We can make it to Camelback Mountain and back by dark with time to spare. No problem." It took only milliseconds for me to make up my mind, put my friend's words above my mother's and grandparents', and head for the hills—right into a real problem.

154

In those days, there were mainly dirt roads on the mountain and many more cacti than houses. We loved the area because of the hills and bumps that became launching pads for us on our bicycles.

As I took one particularly thrilling jump, I lost control of my bike and smashed it right into a cholla cactus near the path. Although I survived the crash without being covered with thorns, the same thing couldn't be said about my front tire. It was flat as a pancake, and I was on foot, far from home.

Needless to say, the streetlight in front of my house was glowing in the dark like an evil eye by the time I walked up with my bicycle. I knew that the excuse of a flat tire wouldn't get me out of trouble this time, and sure enough, I was sent back to my grandfather's room for a spanking.

After the spanking was over, I was moping around in the kitchen when my grandmother told me to get my grandfather for dinner. "No way!" I said. But with one look and the threat of another spanking, I slunk down the hall to knock on his door.

As I came up to his room, the door was slightly ajar. In our house, it was a rule that we knocked on a door before entering someone's room. Because it was already partly open, however, I slowly pushed it the rest of the way and saw my grandfather sitting on his bed, crying.

"Grandfather, what's wrong?" I said.

As he looked up from the bed with tears streaming down his face, he motioned for me to come over to him. He wrapped his arms around me. "John," he said, "I love you boys so much. I want you to grow up to be the kind of men I'd be proud of. I hate to have to spank you, but you need to learn to respect what your mother says. Please listen to her and make me proud of you."

Both my grandfather and I stood there crying and hugging each other. It was the first time in all my young life I had heard my grandfather say he loved me, much less that it wasn't easy for him to spank us. I was so moved by knowing that the boundaries he enforced in my life were for my own good that I didn't want to do anything to hurt him

155

again for the rest of my life—and I'm sure I succeeded for at least a week!

Even though I didn't shape up overnight, there was a dramatic decrease in the number of spankings I received after that day. I knew too much about my grandfather's heart and his love for me to want to hurt him again. I also knew he was right in wanting me to follow my mother's rules instead of a friend's ill-founded advice.

Less than a year later, my grandfather died while we were all at home, but his words and those few moments in his room remain as vivid in my memory as if they happened yesterday. So, too, can be your words of love that call a child to please God and his parents before other people in his life.

PLEASING OTHERS CAN COME AT TOO GREAT A PRICE

Not marking out boundaries for whom your children try to please or what they'll do to gain someone else's approval leaves them wide open to attack. Children who have the deepest needs for acceptance often go to the greatest lengths to receive it. Pleasing others no matter what the price proves most costly to themselves.

Parents who sense an unmet need for acceptance in a child's life or who have a son or daughter who has a natural bent to be a "people pleaser" have a special responsibility to provide helpful boundaries for them. What happens if they don't? Just look at Saul in the Old Testament. By wanting to please the wrong people, he ended up destroying the most precious relationships he had, those with his son and the Lord.

Above Pleasing People

Saul never learned an important lesson parents should teach their children. First and foremost, we are to please God by honoring His Word. There's a very good reason for

God says we should do with our lives keeps us inside the fence where we are safe and secure. Every time we disobey God's Word or listen to another's voice (even our own) that contradicts the Lord's, we've stepped outside the fence and are on the path toward a forbidding wilderness.

Twice, Saul forgot whom he should be most concerned with pleasing, and each time it took him outside the protective fence of God's security. One time, to be successful in battle, Saul was specifically ordered by Samuel to stay put and wait for him to offer sacrifices (1 Samuel 13:8ff.). However, when his troops began to grumble and some began to desert, Saul caved in to peer pressure and offered the sacrifices himself. Another time, he was ordered to destroy an incredibly wicked, diseased city and its inhabitants and animals, but he listened to the people instead and left the best of the spoils intact for his soldiers (1 Samuel 15:12ff.).

Trying to please other people instead of God can land us in hot water. It certainly did for Saul. It damaged his relationship with his son, Jonathan,[1] and it crushed his relationship with the Lord. Samuel put it this way: "Because you have rejected the word of the LORD./He also has rejected you from being king" (1 Samuel 15:23).

How can you help your children answer the question "Whom do I want to please?" and have them put God's name and your name at the top of the list? How can you help them have a fighting chance to face the often overpowering words *peer pressure?* We know this is going to sound trite, but sometimes what works best is getting back to the basics—actively loving them and helping them see how much they are loved by God.

> **The worse your relationship is with your children, the lower the fence against peer pressure that you provide for them.**

When Paul wanted the Corinthian believers to shape up and quit trying to please the immoral crowd in their city, he pointed out how much their heavenly Father loved them: "You were bought at a price." (Literally, he told them, "You have been bought with honor."[2]) "Therefore glorify God in your body" (1 Corinthians 6:20).

If you want your children to think of you when it comes to whom they should please, you must major in loving them. Your best defense against peer pressure later in the kids' lives is building a great relationship with them when they're young. The worse your relationship is with your children, the lower the fence against peer pressure that you provide for them. However, when children know they are loved, they can be encouraged to stay within the limits of your words and please you and their Lord first.

There are two other questions that can give you specific help in setting up positive, protective boundaries.

Questions #3 and #4: "What Should I Accomplish?" and "Where Am I in Accomplishing My Goals?"

Do you know the most important goals your children have today and how to help them reach those goals? Do you know what type of people they are attracted to as friends, and have you helped them set their dating standards? Are your children taking responsibility for or accomplishing tasks today that can give them a positive sense of their abilities in the future? If you don't help your children identify what they should accomplish and then help them reach goals that are important to them, you leave them without a protective fence. To put it another way, if you don't help your children set their schedules or make decisions on what is truly important, *someone else will.*

From celebrities on TV to negative influences at school, there is no lack of people who will set a direction children should follow, even if it differs from what you know is the way they should go. Children like to accomplish things and become proficient at some undertaking. If you simply turn your head instead of getting to know their likes and goals, they may become all-state drug takers instead of all-state band members.

When you set a boundary for what your child accomplishes,

you should keep a loving balance between the child's real abilities and what you might envision or want for him. Sammy's father never took his son's feelings into consideration when he set goals for his life, and his actions nearly destroyed his son.

When Goals Become Burdens

Sammy was larger than many boys his age in grade school and exceptionally gifted in sports, but he didn't like competitive sports at all. That dislike grew into a definite hatred as his father had him down at the local park every night, throwing a football to him or hitting him grounders to develop his talents. After all, with all Sammy's talent, his father was raising his own retirement plan if his son one day got into the pros.

Sammy made it as far as a ward in a psychiatric hospital. Along the way he picked up all-state honors in high-school football and a full scholarship to a major college, but during his junior year he cracked emotionally under the conflicting pressures within himself and never played a down of football again.

Exaggerated expectations can cripple a child. You should make every effort to help him set realistic goals he can try to reach. Recently, I did this very thing with my (Gary's) son Michael.

Inspired by many of the pro athletes he's met in the conferences John and I speak at, Mike decided last year he wanted to be a football player. This past spring, long before he tried out for the football team, Mike let me know in a number of ways that his goal was to make first string.

So one afternoon we sat down together for almost four hours and drew out a conditioning and skill-building plan as Mike had watched me do with his brother, Greg. All I did was ask Mike some questions like these: "How well do you want to do on the team?" "What do you think is your best skill today? Running? Passing? Kicking?" "How much time would you be willing to put into developing the skills that need strengthening? A half hour a day? An hour a week? Once a month?" "Do you want me to ask you once a week how you're doing with your running and passing? Once a month?''

Mike wanted to improve several areas over the spring and summer. These things gave him a goal he could shoot for and a positive feeling that he was organized in his efforts and not simply shooting in the dark. We came up with a plan of exercises and practice drills that was designed to help him get in better shape and improve his passing and running skills.

That's an example of how I helped him figure out what he should accomplish. By taking a goal in his life and working with him to set up a plan to reach it, I was establishing a positive boundary so that other things wouldn't crowd out his goal. Then I helped him evaluate where he was in accomplishing that goal.

Taking Time to Inspect Their Efforts

If you do it in a loving way, a child feels special when you inspect what she does. What parent hasn't taken his child to the swimming pool when the child is learning to go off the diving board and heard one hundred times, ''Watch me!'' as she goes off the end? However, if you're too critical in your appraisal of her abilities, you can drive her away and make her efforts seem like bondage, not a building time. A child who knows you care enough about her to ask the hard questions in a loving way tackles a task feeling loved, and her self-worth is raised in the process.

Mike and I decided together that I should ask him once a week during the off-season how he was doing at meeting his goals. We also decided together what penalty, if any, he wanted me to impose if he didn't do what he agreed to do. Finally, we put everything we talked about in the form of a short contract that we both signed.[3] He knew in advance when I'd ask him about his goals, and he was involved in setting up any discipline there would be if he didn't meet them.

Norma and I have done the same kinds of things with Kari concerning the type of person she wants to date, with Greg on the vocation he wants to choose, and with each of the children concerning their spiritual goals and ministry aspirations.

Leaving a child without any boundaries for what he could or should accomplish with the gifts God has given him can lead to ruin for the child. We can't tell you how many adults have lamented the fact that their parents never took the time to help them be really successful in at least one area of their lives, and that has always been a discouraging factor for them. Others have discovered the truth in the old adage "an idle mind is the devil's workshop."

By setting up helpful fences around a child, you can help him gain a sense of success he can carry with him to adulthood. Building loving boundaries gives you a chance to be involved in his life in a positive way as you teach him responsibility and show him what goals are really important.

WHO'S MANNING THE GATES?

As we close this discussion of the importance of establishing boundaries and the types that are most helpful in honoring children and attaching high value to them, we'd like to ask, Who's manning the gates of the fences that surround your children?

Your goal should be to teach your children responsibility and the ability to self-monitor those things that should come into their lives and those things that should be removed. Yet for those of you who are still in the process of teaching your children about making wise choices and decisions, you risk having a mess if you let them man the gates. That's not to knock your children, but simply to point out the reality of what happens when they make decisions about things in which you should be involved. Leave a child in charge of the gates that enter or leave his world, and he may follow a junk food diet or fall prey to the lure of drugs.

Until children can establish a value system for themselves that reflects God's view of life, they are in danger of being controlled by their emotions or their glands. Loving them enough to set up protective boundaries gives them the gift of honor. Teach them to honor God's boundaries in their lives as well, and you do the best you can to build and protect their self-worth.

We've now looked at several ways in which you can raise your children's value. Next we'll consider an aspect of honor that can stretch across thousands of miles and through decades of time, namely, building positive loyalties.

CHAPTER THIRTEEN

Building Positive Loyalties: Part 1

Children are incredibly loyal. I (John) learned this first-hand when my brother and I decided to quit kindergarten after the first day.

Growing up in a home with three boys, we learned nursery rhymes that had undergone certain editorial changes. In particular, we were taught that little boys were made of "sugar and spice and everything nice" and little girls were made of "snips and snails and puppydog tails." This didn't present a problem at home, but it caused major problems at kindergarten.

Like all children with older brothers or sisters, my twin brother and I had longed for the day we would get to attend school. However, we had no more than sat down on our first morning of kindergarten than the teacher began reading a nursery rhyme. When she read that little boys were made of all manner of disgusting things, our hands shot up. The teacher had the nursery rhyme all wrong! Then, as if it weren't enough that the teacher didn't know how to recite nursery rhymes correctly, the entire class had it wrong, too! We were fit to be tied, and we stormed out of the room when class was over.

"We're never going back to kindergarten," we announced with firm resolve when we got home that afternoon. We went to great lengths to question the intelligence of that teacher and every child at that "dumb" school. Who cared how the rhyme was actually written? We were loyal to our family's way of doing things, and we *knew* how it should be read.

Now that we've grown up, it's easy to see how "childish" we were in clinging unquestioningly to what we were taught. The only problem is that when it comes to family loyalties, many of us never grow up. Like a cookie-cutter pattern, traits and actions often get passed down without question from generation to generation. Take children who are abused, for example.

Children who grow up experiencing terrible abuses often repeat the very same patterns they endured. In fact, one study noted that over 90 percent of parents who abused their children were themselves abused when they were young.[1]

Whether it's something cute, such as misquoting a nursery rhyme, or something crushing, such as experiencing the trauma of abuse, we all have a deep inner drive that calls us to be loyal to parental patterns and repeat what we've learned at home. Family loyalties are those positive or negative patterns, attitudes, or actions that we saw in the family as we were growing up, and by habit, compulsion, or choice, we're consciously or unconsciously repeating them today.

BRINGING TO LIGHT INVISIBLE LINES OF LOYALTY

Family loyalties are the cords from our past that pull on us to put into practice what we have seen repeated by our parents or other close family members. They are the bottomline ways of living what we "caught" by watching our parents on a daily basis, not necessarily what we were "taught" by their words.

A nonnegotiable parents need to understand is that *lines of loyalty are set up in every home*. The only option they have is whether their results will be beneficial or destructive.

Positive loyalties are those patterns and deeply ingrained

ways of thinking and acting that call people back to God's light should they stray; they are the bonds that continue to link a child and her parents in their old age—even if there is no inheritance at stake. Positive loyalties are the patterns that, in spite of all the fighting and squabbling when children are young, draw siblings back together with a special love as they grow older.

Negative loyalties are those hurtful parental patterns that have just as much sway over a person. They're manifested in people like the alcoholic son who swore to himself and to God that he would never take to drinking like his dad; the daughter who, just like her mother, marries for the fourth time and has as her unwritten motto, When the going gets tough, get another partner; the man who, like his father, can never quite seem to be convinced "beyond a reasonable doubt" that there is a God he will answer to one day.

Lines of loyalty in a family act like invisible fibers that can be incredibly strong, strands that stretch across thousands of miles and through decades of time. As we'll discuss in the next few chapters, there's both a positive side and a dark side to family loyalties.

We'd like to offer you four ways to enrich your children's lives by building positive loyalties. Understanding and applying the elements of God's loyal-love is a great place to start and a great way to honor your loved ones.

BUILDING POSITIVE FAMILY LOYALTIES

What exactly do we mean when we use the word *loyalty?* When you think of loyalty, you may picture your faithful dog, a couple celebrating their fiftieth wedding anniversary, or even the Royal Mounted Police. My (John's) first thought when I hear this word is of my older brother, Joe.

Joe is the embodiment of a perfect older brother. Always there when you need him, always interested in what you're doing, always the first one there and the last one to leave on moving day, always ready to listen to you or give his advice, and most of all, he's simply always there.

I have absolutely no doubt that if I had a flat tire in New York in the middle of the night and called Joe at his home in San Diego to ask him to give me a hand, he'd be on the next plane if he thought I needed him. That's the way he is. He's proved it over and over throughout the years by his committed love and his steadfast ways.

Joe's loyal-love for his brothers is a small reflection of God's loyal-love for us. One of the greatest benefits of being a Christian is knowing that God's love holds on to us—no matter what. Joe's love is a small picture of God's carving out an unchanging commitment to His children. C. S. Lewis once put it this way:

> *The great thing to remember is that, though our feelings come and go, His love for us does not. It is not wearied by our sins, or our indifference; and therefore, it is quite relentless in its determination that we shall be cured of those sins, at whatever cost to us, at whatever cost to Him.*[2]

In the Scriptures, we can see the positive side of God's commitment to love us in the concept of His loyal-love for His children. Translated in many places as "lovingkindness," the Hebrew word *hesed* speaks of lasting bonds of kindness or loyalty.[3]

Wrapped around this key concept are the twin ideas of love and loyalty.[4] This love speaks specifically of being tender and merciful, and this commitment is pictured as steadfast and unconditional. Let's look closer at these two elements of God's love for His children. In doing so, we can get a picture of the way positive lines of loyalty are developed.

THE ELEMENTS OF GOD'S LOYAL-LOVE

1. Tenderness Is a Key to Providing Positive Loyalty Bonds.

There's a powerful principle at work throughout the Scriptures. We can catch a glimpse of it when we read:

THE GIFT OF HONOR

A soft answer turns away wrath,
But a harsh word stirs up anger.
(Proverb 15:1)

By long forbearance a ruler is persuaded,
And a gentle tongue breaks a bone.
(Proverb 25:15)

A soft or gentle answer can stand up to a heated argument. Persistently making gentle requests can break the backbone of the most insensitive ruler. These verses are pointing to what needs to take place in our families.

When it comes to setting down healthy lines of loyalty, we honor our children when we bring gentleness and tenderness into our homes. In many places in the Bible, the word *loyal-love* is translated "tenderness, mercy, and lovingkindness."[5] When God bound Himself to His people, He did so with gentle bonds of affection and caring. This is important because children who grow up with loads of tender loving care can't help carrying into later life the stamp, "I'm valuable."

Have you ever had a treasured family heirloom that rated special attention and protection? Jimmy's parents did. In fact, their house was filled with antiques and art treasures that made nearly every room off limits to a healthy, growing boy.

Of Less Value than a Vase. Jimmy was constantly criticized for touching this or picking up that. His normal boyish curiosity became such a test of wills that his parents would tie him in the family room with a length of rope to keep him from getting into trouble or breaking something.

Eventually, Jimmy seemed to get better about being around the costly treasures. Whether it was the repeated lectures he received or, more likely, the repeated spankings, he seemed resigned to the fact that the house was filled with things that he shouldn't go near.

To be sure, Jimmy seemed to become increasingly withdrawn and tense, but at least he was showing some respect for his parents' precious possessions that is, until one tragic day.

Jimmy's parents drove down to the neighborhood store one afternoon when he was in fourth grade. When they came home, they were greeted with a shocking sight. Little Jimmy had gone into his bedroom and put on his new pair of cowboy boots. Then with systematic persistence, he had gone through every room in the house, kicking and smashing to pieces every "precious" item he could get his hands on.

Little Jimmy knew that there were items in his house that rated special attention, and he also knew that he wasn't one of them. Every day he walked among vases and pictures that called out to him with mocking voices, "We're more valuable than you are. We're handled more gently than you!" That knowledge had simmered within him until it boiled over and resulted in his aggressive behavior. At nine years of age, Jimmy began what would turn into six years of psychiatric treatment at two different hospitals to deal with his problems, problems that were a reflection of how little he was valued by his parents.

Children need to know that they are valuable treasures to parents. This is at the heart of our definition of honor. One effective way parents can communicate honor is to handle them with tenderness.

Priceless Treasures in Our Home. The next time you get angry with your children, try thinking of them as precious antique vases. How likely would you be to pick up a priceless vase in your living room and shake it around? The value you attach to it would make you check your behavior. The same thing should be true of your living treasures.

Are there things inside or outside your house that your children see you polishing, mowing, pruning, playing with, or spending time over that appear to be more valuable than they are? We know of one young woman who is convinced that her mother cares more for her pet poodle than she does for her. Why? Because of the difference in her mother's facial expressions and tone of voice. With the poodle, she is soft and tender. With her daughter, her face becomes strict and expressionless, and her words have a cold chill of disapproval.

How tender are you with your children? Does your tone of voice reflect the value you want to communicate to them? Do you touch them and tell them how special they are to you? Do you respond in gentleness to them when they're hurting? Are you willing to ask your spouse or a close family friend to express an opinion about how well you're doing in this area?

Children remember acts of tenderness with striking clarity. Unfortunately, they are just as good at remembering angry words and insensitive actions. Fathers in particular need to understand how damaging angry words can be. One research study concluded that a hostile, angry father leaves the greatest emotional scars on a child's life.[6]

It doesn't take an elaborate birthday party or a European vacation to convince a child he is special. Providing him with a gentle hug or a soft, loving tone of voice can do wonders toward building his self-worth.

No parent is perfect. There will be times when you'll speak out in anger. There will be other times when you'll discipline them with only punishment, not principle, in mind. But if you'll demonstrate tenderness on a *consistent basis*, you'll see positive lines of loyalty attach to your children's lives. We recommend actions like these:

- Gently admit to your children when you know you've been wrong to them. This goes a long way toward building self-worth.
- Take time to squeeze their arm or give them a hug.
- Watch or soften your tone of voice, if necessary, when they make a mistake.
- Listen carefully; don't lecture.
- Cry with them about something they hurt over.
- Write them a letter that expresses your love and commitment.
- Pray with them about a past or upcoming trying event.

Treating children with tenderness doesn't mean that you wrap them in cotton. Neither does it mean that righteousness goes out the window and permissiveness comes in. There will be times when you'll have to discipline them firmly, and other times when you'll have to let them learn life's hard lessons for themselves. But children will go away from home feeling valuable if they're treated consistently with tender care. And they'll find themselves treating others with the value they themselves received.

2. A Covenant of Love Is a Second Key to Providing Positive Lines of Loyalty.

Have you ever watched a television documentary on a mountain-climbing expedition? One thing you'll always spot is a length of rope that links the climbers together. Although it may get in the way at times and become a burden during the climb, you'll notice that none of the climbers is about to take it off. That bond can become a life line should they slip and fall.

Children need consistent lines of loyal-love from you to give them the security and courage to launch out in life. The knowledge that there's always a life line of love if they need it can make all the difference. How can you provide this? By patterning your love after the second element of God's loyal-love.

We've already seen that tenderness is a key way God builds in positive loyalties. Another aspect of His loyal-love is that it is linked with a covenant He makes with us. The original meaning of the Old Testament word *covenant* is to "bind" or "tie together."[7] *When God wanted to communicate how highly He valued His children, He did so by binding Himself to them in the form of a contract or covenant.* "Therefore know that the LORD your God, He is God, the faithful God who keeps covenant and mercy for a thousand generations" (Deuteronomy 7:9).

The security that comes with knowing we are lovingly tied to our heavenly Father, even when we stumble and fall, is a tremendous gift. And it is nearly as important for us to feel the same way about our parents' love for us. For one thing, knowing we are forever bound in love to our parents can free us from the constant burden of having to prove we're acceptable and the fear that we're not.

Climbing without a Life Line. An interesting study examined the effects of parenting on a number of top-level executives.[8] The men and women were divided into two study groups that were later compared with each other.

One group was comprised of "Type A" individuals. They were men and women who were consumed with time pressures, or "hurry sickness." They were very competitive, had an intense need to accumulate more and more material possessions, and recorded high levels of hostility and aggression.

The second group contained "Type B" individuals. These people exhibited the opposite of "Type A" traits. They would often take time to relax, were basically content with the levels attained in their personal, business, and financial lives, and had little hostility or anger.

Two crystal-clear results surfaced in this study. First, "Type A" men and women scored at the top of the charts in feeling insecure about themselves. Even when they were surrounded by impressive business and personal accomplishments—often much more significant than those accomplished by people in the "B" group—they had a deep, inner fear that they would lose it all.

Where did such a fear come from? From the second major finding in the study: "Type A" men and women were at the bottom in viewing themselves as having received unconditional acceptance and high self-esteem from their parents.

The connection is not to be overlooked. Leave a person to climb the mountains of life without the life line of unconditional acceptance, and watch the problems mount. For many, getting to the top of one mountain peak only causes them to look up and see another, higher pinnacle they must climb. And if they don't burn out emotionally in the struggle, they are four times more likely to crumble physically through coronary artery disease.[9]

Not long ago we watched a national evening news broadcast profile the world's greatest woman triathlete. When she was asked what motivated her to swim several miles, ride a bicycle race of up to one hundred miles, and then run a full twenty-six-mile marathon—all without stopping—her reply was a window to her heart. She said, "I guess I am just one of those people who never grew up feeling very valuable. Even though it's difficult, when I go out and win a race, I guess I feel better about myself . . . at least for a while."[10]

We see more and more adults today who are out on the track of life trying just as hard to raise that "perfect" child, gain that next promotion, get that book accepted by a publisher, or drive that certain car to work. Most are missing the second element of God's loyal-love, a strong sense of being secure in the love of someone special. That someone special ought to be Mom or Dad.

Children get an incredible sense of security from knowing that they are tied to parents who are committed to their best interests for life. When the time comes that their feet are pulled out from under them and they are sent tumbling headlong, having a lifeline of loyal-love to break their fall and pull them to a place of safety is better than owning gold.

You can begin today to build feelings of security into your children by actions such as these:

- Take a few minutes each evening to ask them how their day went. (Usually, you'll get more information from your daughter than your son, but it's equally important to ask both.)
- Attend their games, concerts, and open houses.
- Demonstrate love for your spouse in front of the children.
- Put down in writing or record on a cassette ten reasons you're proud of each child, and share them in a special time together.
- Commend them on their effort, even when they lose a game or do poorly on an exam.
- Give them a plaque that's inscribed with your lifetime commitment to your spouse and your children.

LEAVING CHILDREN WITH LOVING-KINDNESS

Children who are willing to risk new challenges and relationships know intuitively that there are lines of security to catch them if they fall. To be able to leave home in a healthy way, they need the reassurance that only unconditional love brings.

Just how much impact do acts of loving-kindness, actions that display God's loyal-love, have on children? Even small acts of tenderness and kindness can leave lasting memories that affirm the value of individuals. General Dwight Eisenhower learned this in the war-torn streets of London.

During World War II, London took a terrible beating at the hands of the German Luftwaffe. Nearly every night, the sirens would wail, and spotlights would pierce the black sky trying to find the German bombers. Before the planes returned to their bases in France, dozens more English men, women, and children would be dead, injured, or homeless. Many orphans roamed the streets months after the air raids stopped.

One day, in preparing for the invasion of France on D-day, General Eisenhower decided to walk to his headquarters instead of having his staff car drive him the few blocks. As he passed a bakery along the way, he noticed two young, poorly dressed boys with their noses pressed up against the window. The delicious smells of fresh bread and pastries floated out of the shop and wrapped themselves around anyone who walked by. The general could see the object of their attention—chocolate donuts.

While a few members of his staff looked on with skepticism, Ike stopped and had his orderly purchase a dozen donuts. The general bent down and gently placed a sack with a half-dozen donuts in each child's hands. Understandably, a look of disbelief swept over their faces. Looking up at the commander of the Allied forces, one of the young boys asked in a halting voice, "Mister, are you God?"

Our Lord knew that tenderness and kindness leave lasting bonds on His loved ones' hearts. That's why He will remember even a cup of water we give to others in His name (Matthew 10:42). That's also why the Psalms are filled with praise for a God who is merciful and forgives our sins, and the gospels are filled with the story of a Savior who loved us all the way to the cross while we were yet sinners.[11]

CHAPTER FOURTEEN

Building Positive
Loyalties: Part 2

We've looked at two ways to build positive loyalties in children's lives, strands that can provide loving support and a life line for them to rely on. In this chapter, we'll consider two more crucial ways in which nurturing positive loyalties can honor children and help them increase their sense of self-worth.

3. The Freedom to Question Is a Third Key to Providing Positive Loyalty Bonds.

We've been intrigued by the finding that some of the healthiest homes are those where children are allowed the freedom to ask questions—even of Mom and Dad. That may not sit well with some parents whose favorite line is, "Because I *told* structively can give children a sense of confidence, competence, and independence and increase their love and respect for their parents.

In one major study, elementary-school boys and girls were asked to agree or disagree with the statement, "Children should never question the thinking of their parents." Researchers discovered that students who scored high on feelings of personal worth *disagreed* 5 to 1 with the statement, while 90 percent of the students who felt of little value *agreed* by the same margin.[1]

One family expert writes,

We find that the healthy family is notable for the high level of activity of its individual members, strong-minded parents dealing with independent, assertive children, stricter enforcement of more stringent demands and greater possibilities for open dissent and disagreement.

This picture brings to mind firm convictions, frequent and possibly strong exchanges and people who are capable and ready to assume leadership and who will not be treated casually or disrespectfully.[2]

When I (Gary) first read this statement, I thought someone had been listening in on some of the dinner conversations around our kitchen table! From the time our children were young, we've given them the freedom to ask us straightforward questions, and they've taken the opportunity to do so, just as Mike did the other day.

During the winter months when people across the country are shivering from the cold, those of us who live in Arizona enjoy sunny, warm, near-perfect weather. Something else we get to enjoy is the number of relatives and friends who come out to bask in the perfect weather with us.

Recently, we received the news that an old family friend would be coming out to visit us for several weeks. As we talked about it around the dinner table one night, I said, "Nancy can stay in your room, Mike, and you can sleep on the couch in the family room." This seemed like a perfectly good arrangement to me, and I really wasn't bringing up the subject for debate. But I noticed that Mike became quiet and began to look down at his plate.

"What's the matter?" I asked.

Mike looked at me and said, "Dad, the last three times we've had people stay with us, they've stayed in my room, not Greg's or Kari's. Why am I always the one who has to give up my room? Is it because I'm the youngest?"

There are a number of "typical" responses a parent (or I) could have made, such as:

*I can't believe how selfish you are, Mike! Do you
want me to call Nancy and tell her that you can't
stand her and you want her to sleep on the couch?*
or
*You're not a lawyer, young man. I won't stand for
being cross-examined in my own home! You're sleeping on the couch, or you can sleep in the garage!*

Thankfully, I didn't use either response. Because Norma
and I have encouraged the children to ask questions throughout their growing-up years, we took the time as a family to
talk about where Nancy should stay.

With a few well-chosen words, I could have lectured
Mike about "doing what he was told" and closed his spirit
in the process.[3] But by honoring his question as honest and
valid, we grew closer together as a family. The result was
that we took turns sleeping on the couch.

For some reason, questions can be threatening. This is
particularly true when they come from our children. Perhaps this is because questions can demonstrate our fallibil-
ity in a flash or threaten to expose the fact that we're not
perfect decision makers. Yet the more healthy the relationship, the more willing people are to ask and answer even
difficult questions.

We see this frequently in troubled marriages. Many times
a husband and wife have learned the hard way what *not* to
talk about simply by asking questions. Others have received only icy stares from their mates when they uttered
the off-limits question "Why?"

Having the security to allow your children to ask questions
can go a long way toward building value into their lives. For
some children, never allowing them to question you can teach
them to drive their true feelings underground, cause them to
have feelings of anger, lead them to challenge you on everything, or encourage them to develop manipulative tendencies.
Others can stay tied up emotionally in cold steel chains,
afraid or unwilling to challenge or change something you
have said, even if it proves to be unbiblical or wrong.

We want to be sure we're communicating clearly the
kinds of questions we're talking about. We're not talking

about putting up with whining over regular chores ("Mom, I took the trash out once *last* week") or debating moral issues when God is crystal clear in His Word. There are and should be nonnegotiables in every household.[4]

However, for some parents, allowing their children to ask legitimate questions is equivalent to someone's turning the Ten Commandments into the Ten Suggestions. "This is my house, and this is the way my family does things. Period." No questions asked, no questions allowed. And that's unfortunate, not to mention unbiblical. As one person said about his father, "He may have not been right all the time, but he was never wrong!"

Our heavenly Father has always given His children the right to ask the hard questions and has felt free to ask them Himself. (Remember the hard questions He put to Adam and Eve in the Garden and to Cain?)[5] One reason He inspires such loyalty in those who love Him is that He's secure in His identity and can let us ask our most difficult questions.

Listen to the psalmist's penetrating words:

> *O God, why have You cast us off forever?*
> *Why does Your anger smoke against*
> *the sheep of Your pasture?*
> . . . .
> *O God, how long will the adversary reproach?*
> *Will the enemy blaspheme Your name forever?*
> *Why do You withdraw Your hand,*
> *even Your right hand?*
> *Take it out of Your bosom*
> *and destroy them.*
>
> (Psalm 74:1, 10–11)

Then listen to our Lord's words: "My God, My God, why have You forsaken Me?" (Matthew 27:46).

The more freedom you give your children to be open and honest with you, the higher you build their worth. When children ask a legitimate question and you give them the stock answer from Parenting 101, "Because I said so, that's good enough," you can leave them with more than their original question. You can also leave them with

    a) a feeling their question was stupid

    b) anger over being denied access to your reasoning process

    c) the conclusion that you are too busy with "important" things to take the time to explain something to your "unimportant" children

    d) all of the above

In all likelihood, the lower a parent's self-worth, the more difficulty he's going to have with questions from his children. Such a parent has too much to prove to himself and too much fear of looking bad to handle the "hot potato" questions a grade-schooler can raise about staying up past her normal bedtime or a junior-high girl can ask about sex.

Instead of laying down lines of loyalty based on how loud you can yell, build greater security into your children by allowing them to ask legitimate questions. If your kids are of high enough value to deserve being honored, they should be given the opportunity to ask questions.

TWO STEPS BACKWARD, ONE BIG STEP FORWARD

4. Understanding Our Own Lines of Loyalty Is a Fourth Key to Providing Positive Loyalty Bonds.

The fourth key to providing positive lines of loyalty for children comes about as we take the time to reflect on and understand the lines of loyalty that are still present with our own parents. Understandably, this isn't always easy to do.

Some of us may pretend to be like the emperor with the invisible clothes. No matter how much we may protest that we're unaffected by our parents or past, the stark reality lays naked before others who know us well. Take Bill, for example.

Bill grew up with his mother and sister in a single-parent

home. Although they were a very loving family, something happened once a month that has affected Bill all his life—bill-paying time. As in many single-parent homes, finances were very tight for Bill's family. And each month as his mother sat down to pay the bills, a black cloud would seem to settle over the household. Whether it was the "dumb" electric bill or the "dumb" charge card balance that set her off, for two days the kids knew it was best to spend time at their friends' houses and stay out of Mom's way.

Can you guess what's a major problem in Bill's home now that he's grown up and gotten married? You're right—paying bills. Even though Bill has a high-paying job and a fairly frugal lifestyle, he makes life miserable for everyone in the household at the end of the month.

All that is not to say that we bring only negative lines of loyalty into our later relationships, however. Sarah is an example of someone who remains loyal to a helpful family pattern her parents set down for her. Sarah grew up in a home where the welcome mat was always out for missionaries home on furlough or others in need. Three times when Sarah was young, her parents brought in unwed mothers and loved and counseled them through their pregnancies and deliveries.

Today, Sarah possesses a sensitivity and willingness to care for others that's beautiful to see. Sacrificing some personal comfort and needs in order to help others was second nature as she was growing up, and she has carried that tendency into her adult married life.

All of us enter into marriage carrying some of our past, which also affects our roles as parents. Successful husbands and wives, fathers and mothers, take the time to bring these powerful factors to light.

Several years ago, I (John) interviewed for an associate pastor position at a growing, vibrant church. Interviews are often like courtships, and I wasn't sure if I would get the "real scoop" during my visit or an unrealistic picture of what was happening. However, all my fears were dispelled in the first meeting I had with the search committee and the associate pastor who would become my supervisor. The pastor volunteered these words of advice: "John, like any church, we've got a few skeletons in the closet. However, the thing that makes this church different is that we can open the door and talk about them.''

The same thing needs to take place in our families. It doesn't do any good to leave positives *or* negatives buried in the closets of our minds. To be free to build value into our children, we must be aware of the factors pulling on us from the past.

To help you discern some of these lines of loyalty in your own life, take the time to finish the following statements before you go on.

Growing Up in My Family

A. In my family, the way we handled money was to . . .
   The way I handle money today is to . . .

B. In my family, the place our spiritual life held . . .
   Today my spiritual life is . . .

C. In my family, the kind of job my father/mother had . . .
   The kind of job I have now is . . .

D. In my family, the way we were disciplined as children was . . .
   The way I discipline my children is . .

E. In my family, in regard to hospitality, you could say that we were . . .
   For me today, hospitality is . . .

F. In my family, when it came to expressing affectionate words and hugs, we . . .
   My comfort in being affectionate with my spouse and family today is . . .

G. In my family, anger was . . .
   The way I handle my anger with my spouse and children is . . .

H. In my family, when it came to honesty, . . .
   When it comes to honesty in my personal life, . . .

I. In my family, . . . was sometimes carried to an extreme
   In my own life, I tend to carry . . . to an extreme.

J. In my home when I was growing up, we moved
seldom ____ never ____ often ____.

My family has changed houses
seldom ____ never ____ often ____.

In many cases, we can give thanks for the things we repeat from the past. But like Bill, if we become aware of emotional storm clouds that spring up only because it "always used to rain that way in our family," we do ourselves and our children a favor to honestly confront our family "traditions."

In the book of Proverbs, Solomon wrote, "The wisdom of the prudent is to understand his way,/But the folly of fools is deceit."[6] Giving thought to how lines of loyalty from our past still affect us is certainly wise, because it can help us be open to God's Spirit and build value into our children.

We've looked at four ways we can build positive lines of loyalty into our children. These practices can call forth their affection for a lifetime and give them security and support even after we're gone.

By applying each factor, a parent goes a long way toward building positive loyalties into his children. On the other hand, the "casual observer" type of parent runs the risk of seeing his children gravitate toward the dark side of family loyalties. That's a place as cold and lifeless as the dark side of the moon, where dishonor and low self-worth dwell. Let's enter the front door and look at five different homes where dishonor and low self-worth dominate.

CHAPTER FIFTEEN

Understanding the Dark Side of Family Loyalties: Part 1

It would be wonderful if every child grew up in a home where positive lines of loyalty and God's loyal-love abounded. Unfortunately, that isn't always the case. As difficult as it may be to admit, we need to realize that there is a darker side to family loyalties as well.

In the last two chapters, we looked at actions parents can take today to build positive habits and characteristics that children will have a natural tendency to repeat tomorrow. Negative loyalties take shape in much the same way. With their big, perceptive eyes, children can pick up negative patterns from parents every bit as quickly as positive ones. Some of these bonds can inhibit their ability to develop a healthy self-concept, rob them of joy in the present, and chain them to devaluing patterns from the past. Left untouched and unexplored, these hurtful patterns will be seen again and again, passed down from parent to child.

Sound like too strong a statement? It's been true for generations. "I, the LORD your God, am a jealous God, visiting the iniquity of the fathers on the children to the third and fourth generations of those who hate Me."[1] Ever since Jesus died on the cross, Christians have been freed from the demands of this verse, and God gives us freedom to choose patterns that lead to life. Yet many people never experience freedom from past wrongs. Instead, they hold on to negative patterns with incredible loyalty from generation to generation. They're like people who have an inheritance of a million dollars in the bank, but choose to stand in a poverty line and never write a check against their bulging bank account.

In this chapter and the following one, we depict five homes that tend to produce strong negative lines of loyalty, gripping bonds that we see people struggling with almost on a daily basis. By taking an honest look at these patterns, you can see if any of them are a part of your parenting style—or a part of your past—and take steps to cope with them. Each can wrap around a child and pull him away from feeling valuable. Each dishonors a child and can damage his self-worth. If not brought into the open and dealt with, each has the power to chain a child to a hurtful pattern for a lifetime.

We also offer some practical help and hope to those who may have struggled with negative loyalty bonds for years. Although God's Word can cut even the strongest negative bond, it is far better never to have gone through such an experience.

Confronting negative lines of loyalty isn't easy. These dishonoring practices are powerful, and it's difficult to break free from them. As a way of illustrating their impact, let's look in on a practice that can shed some light on the task before us.

PULLING AGAINST CHAINS FROM THE PAST

From the time we were young, most of us have been told that elephants never forget. Maybe this old adage started because of a particular training method used in India. When a baby elephant has been weaned from its mother, it is driven away from her and chained to a heavy stake. Until the animal's spirit is broken, it will be given neither food nor water.

Elephants are extremely bright, persistent animals, and there is much evidence to suggest that in some ways, they, indeed, never forget. For days many of these young animals will pull against the stake that holds them, rubbing the tethered leg raw in the process. However, we're told that one morning when the trainer wakes up, the struggle is over.

As if the animal has made some final decision, it no longer pulls at the stake, and it never will again. That's why at a circus, you'll often see huge elephants tethered with a rope around their ankles. In an instant, these grown animals could snap their feeble bonds, yet they stay in their place as if secured by heavy chains. Many elephants will rock back and forth as they stand (many do this continuously), but they will never again risk the pain involved in pulling away from what hurt them in the past.

All too often we've seen a similar reaction to negative family loyalties. Growing up in a dishonoring home, many children will initially pull away from painful practices in their homes. Often they make statements like these: "There's no way I'm going to do what my parents did with me when I grow up" or "Things are going to be different when I get out on my own and have my own family" or "I can hardly wait to leave this house!"

However, as they grow older, many of these same people stay chained to the very things they want so desperately not to repeat. After years of struggling, many become so emotionally tired and raw that they quit trying to change those patterns and let the chains from the past confine them.

If you find yourself in any of the examples that follow, please don't lose hope. While relief may not come overnight, we'll show how Christ can remove your chains from the past. With His power you are more than able to break free from them and make sure you don't pass them on to your children.[2]

When you have the courage to bring into His light negative lines of loyalty that have long remained in the shadows, you open yourself to genuine change. Just like your spiritual growth, freedom from these bonds usually comes through days and weeks of gaining understanding of your situation and making daily decisions to believe what God has said.

1. THE DESIGNATED SCAPEGOAT

For the Old Testament Jews, a special ceremony took place every year on the Day of Atonement. Unfortunately, that ceremony reflects what happens in many homes today.

The ceremony worked like this: two goats were chosen by lots, one to be sacrificed, and the other to become a scapegoat. Sacrificing an animal was a familiar part of Old Testament law. But what was the purpose of the scapegoat?

Aaron, the high priest, would gather all the people together and lay his hands on the goat's head. In doing so, he was giving them a symbolic picture that all the sins of the nation had been transferred to the animal.[3] The goat was then driven outside the camp and forced into the wilderness to die.

When Jesus was led outside the city to be crucified and the Father placed our sins upon Him, He became our scapegoat and our lamb of sacrifice.[4] For Israel of old as well as for Christians today, having a scapegoat pictured a meaningful, even glorious event.

Today, because of Christ's death on the cross, the sacrificial system is no longer needed, but unknowingly, some families carry it on anyway. These homes have adopted a scapegoat in the family, someone who shoulders all the blame for an unhealthy family's problems.

Just like the scapegoats of old, children who grow up bearing the brunt of all their family's problems are often discarded and driven away from those they love. Instead of severing the bonds between parent and child, this binds these children tighter to a negative picture of themselves. This type of home scores near-perfect marks in lowering a child's value. Just like Gretta. She was the scapegoat in her family.

Gretta was born during the early days of World War II, and from her first few days of life, she was unjustly labeled as being the cause of every problem in her household. The last of four children, Gretta developed a terrible skin condition shortly after she was born that caused lesions and boils to cover most of her body.

Not only that, but Gretta also had a terrible respiratory

problem that made it hard for her to sleep longer than a few hours at a time and caused her to wake up coughing and choking. She would cry for hours at a time when she was young, and her mother soon was overwhelmed by all the care she required night and day.

Today, many men help with their children, but that wasn't the case in Gretta's era. Because of all the noise around the house from the other children and the stress his wife was under because of Gretta, the father simply spent more and more time away from home.

As the war grew in intensity in Europe and it looked as though the United States would be drawn in, Gretta's father decided he would enlist in the army. Even though he had a minor medical condition that could have kept him out of the service if he chose, he jokingly told his wife that he could still send her a paycheck, but he wouldn't have to listen to Gretta cry and fuss day and night!

After that, things became more and more strained between Gretta and her mother. These problems came to a head on Gretta's second birthday. That was the day the notice came from the War Department announcing that her father had been killed in the battle of Palermo in Italy.

Gretta's mother took the news terribly hard. As a way of dealing with the hurt, she began blaming Gretta for all their problems. None of the other children caused her such grief—only Gretta. None of the others demanded so much time—only Gretta. None of the other children gobbled up so much of the precious money for doctor bills—only Gretta. It wasn't because of Gretta's sisters or brothers that her husband had enlisted and now lay dead on a battlefield—it was Gretta's fault.

A year later, Gretta's mother remarried. However, things didn't improve for Gretta. As time went by, the poor girl grew up feeling she was the sole reason for all the problems in her family.

Her brothers and sisters picked up on their mother's negative attitude toward Gretta and shunned her, blaming her for the fact that their natural father would never return. The stepfather resented the constant medical attention Gretta required to help with her respiratory problems, and he gave her nothing but scorn and contempt. But the things her mother said to her hurt the most.

Gretta's mother had lived an immoral life before she was married. Although she had never been a religious person before her husband's death, she suddenly became interested in the Bible as a way of dealing with the guilt and anger she felt. However, instead of finding help or solace or a personal relationship with Christ, her understanding became twisted, and she found another weapon to use against Gretta. In an emotional outburst one day, Gretta's mother screamed at her, "God gave you to me as punishment for all my sins and all the wrongs I've done!"

While you might think that Gretta would have grown up and moved away without any bonds of attachment to her mother, just the opposite was true. She was attached all right, but it was to a negative image of herself that took years to correct.

Singled Out for Shame

Children who become the scapegoat of the family long for the love and acceptance they never received. Often they act out their low self-worth with outbursts of anger or rebellion. They know deep inside the injustice of being singled out and pushed away from the family, and their intense frustrations can find their way out as behavior problems in school, defiance of authority, and flagrant immorality.

Each of these things was true in Gretta's life and is common in others like her. It's almost as if the person who is labeled the scapegoat makes the unhealthy decision to act out the low worth the family attributes to him or her and thus justify the label.

Gretta acted in this very way. She hated the negative attention she received for her angry temper and rebelliousness, but at least she got some attention when her behavior was bad! To a daughter starved for acceptance, even being the family scapegoat gave her some identity in her home. And now that years have passed and Gretta has her own family, her feelings of low self-worth have kept her from feeling genuinely loved by her husband and have made her far more critical of her children than she wants and needs to be.

Although Gretta's case is dramatic, having a scapegoat in a family is a much too common occurrence. As another example, take Mark, who became the scapegoat in a "blended" family. His new mother was so afraid he would "corrupt" her two sons that he was labeled as a trouble-maker and held at arm's length for years. Always knowing he wasn't accepted, he still longed to have a relationship with his "brothers." Mark grew up feeling terrible that he was such a bad person, even when he knew deep inside he was not.

Consider Sara, whose marriage would carry on to the third generation the family tradition of having a scapegoat. In her great-grandmother's home as well as her grandmother's home, one of the daughters had married outside the family's faith and had been cut off as a result. Now as Sara tried to explain to her parents about her new Christian faith, she, too, was branded a family failure and told to stay away. In each generation that cast out a scapegoat, all the other members of the family would link up even tighter, unwilling for the love of their daughter or sister to penetrate their ranks.

In order to give you hope if you've been the family scapegoat, we'll see later on how Gretta, Mark, and Sara were able to break these negative bonds and be free from many of the negative effects of their hurtful past. However, before we do, let's look in on another home that can tie up children with negative lines of loyalty. This one binds them with imprisoning obligations.

2. IMPRISONING OBLIGATIONS

Label a child as the family scapegoat, and watch how tightly bound he becomes to a negative picture of himself. Smother a child with imprisoning obligations, and a similar thing happens. Children from this type of dishonoring home often become so tightly tied to unrealistic expectations that they are rarely able to travel very far in life on their own. This was true for Wayne, a man who had a dream of moving across the country and starting a business of his own but who faced the reality that negative bonds would only let him go across the street. Tragically, this darker side of family loyalties led him to dishonor and devalue his wife and daughter as well.

Wayne was an only child who grew up on the outskirts of a rural town. His father was gone frequently on business trips and seldom had any time for him when he was at home. However, his mother's attitude toward him was quite different. Because her husband was emotionally distant and traveled so often, she made her son the center of her life. For many years, this was a perfectly good arrangement for Wayne, and his mother became his constant companion and his closest friend.

Wayne often dreamed of leaving the small town he lived in and going to the "big city," and he would frequently tell his mother about this dream. Then when he began to mature, a curious thing happened. While his mother had always been the picture of good health before, her condition now started to deteriorate. She was continually fighting off one ailment or another. And though nothing specific could be diagnosed, her frail condition required ever more attention from her son.

With a brave little smile, his mother would look up from her bed and say to Wayne, "I just don't know what I'd do without you. You're the only thing that makes life worth living for me." Then she would add with a sigh, "But I know you'll need to move on one of these days, and I know I'll get along somehow."

"You're the only thing that makes life worth living for me." Her words were only too true. Wayne *was* her life. Through her manipulative words and actions, she began to lay down strand after strand of negative loyalty bonds. Whether it was reminding him of all the hours she had played with him as a child or how "little time she had left," strands of guilt, like reinforced steel wires, were wrapped around the lines of loyalty that held her son.

At age twenty-six, Wayne married without his mother's

consent. In fact, he marched right into his mother's room and told her that he was finished living his life for her. He and his girlfriend would marry and move to the big city.

Up until the wedding, Wayne felt great about confronting his mother and taking a stand. But almost immediately after the ceremony, he began paying the price. Right after the wedding, his mother fell into a physical collapse, and he had to end his honeymoon three days early and rush back to be with her.

At her bedside, Wayne pleaded with his mother to forgive him for being gone when she needed him so much. The only promises that consoled her were that he would look for a job nearby and that he and his new wife would move into the small house across the street. Of course, he also promised he would visit or call her at least twice a day.

For years, Wayne refused to test his limits and pull again on the chains of negative loyalty that bound him. Often, his anger would surface at having to be over at his mother's house all the time or at having to drop everything to attend to an "emergency" that would turn out to be just another opportunity to have her son over. Yet every time, Wayne swallowed his angry feelings when the shadow of guilt passed over him. After all, he had confronted his mother once before, and his actions "brought on a condition." If he dared to do it again, he feared it might be fatal to her.

In a free country, Wayne was in gripping bondage. Unaware of and unwilling to deal with his misplaced loyalties, he was a prisoner to the negative family bonds that chained him.

The Ripple Effect of Imprisoning Obligations

Wayne certainly suffered over the years, but his wife, Susan, probably did even more. The standing invitation for Wayne to come over to his mother's house didn't include his wife. Many evenings Susan would prepare a nice meal for her husband, only to see him drive in from work and walk across to his mother's for dinner, all without coming into the house to speak to her. Even when Susan was with her husband and her mother-in-law, they often talked around her or about her as though she were a child or wasn't in the room.

The more rigidly a person is tied to his parents, the more difficult it is for him to enter into a full commitment to another person in marriage. And Wayne's loyalty to his mother was so strong that he made no effort to commit himself to his wife. Each time he chose his mother over his wife, Susan's value as a person and as a marriage partner went further down. After ten years of marriage, her self-worth was so low that she consistently had thoughts about taking her life. That's when we first met Susan.

In counseling, Wayne spoke about his mother's illnesses and about how trying to meet her need for attention and affection was like trying to fill a cup with a hole in the bottom. Susan's eyes filled with tears, and she said, "How about me, Wayne? I know your mother has needs, but I'm thirsty, too."

Susan suffered in silence for years, never telling a friend or family member her hurt and disappointment, and that in itself is often a negative form of loyalty. It's often the dark side of family loyalties that keeps a child from telling a teacher or friend that he has been abused or that keeps a wife or husband from crying out for help. It's also the darker side of loyalties that makes it so difficult to treat many alcoholics. Getting each member of the family (particularly the nondrinking husband or wife) to quit protecting the person who is drinking and confront him with the truth is like pulling teeth. Misguided loyalty may "protect" a person for a season, but all too often it prevents a cure.

As we have seen, positive loyalty is crucial to marriage and family relationships and involves doing what is best for the other person, even if that means discipline or confrontation. Yet negative loyalty bonds bind a person to his problems rather than free him from them.

Susan was unwilling to risk her shaky relationship with her husband for no relationship at all. She never spoke with her mother-in-law about the treatment she received, and even though she argued with her husband continually, she was careful to push only so far. With all the buried emotions she felt, she began to experience many symptoms of poor health, just like her mother-in-law. And at long last, she was beginning to get some of Wayne's attention.

These two people experienced two different types of imprisoning obligations. Each shows a different aspect of the darker side of family loyalties, but thankfully, they don't have to be lifelong patterns. As we'll see in a later chapter, when Wayne learned who the Source of Life is and how honoring Him could change his life, positive things began happening in his family that would eventually break those crippling bonds.

In Wayne's home, a dishonoring parent played on the natural tendency a child has to be lovingly loyal to his parents. How tragic it was for her that in looking for life in her son, she missed out on knowing the only true Source of Life, and she nearly ruined her son's life and marriage as well.

For Wayne and for many people we see in counseling today, growing up with imprisoning obligations can cause them to develop a negative sense of loyalty. Afraid of losing that "special place" they have with their parents, they accept calling them four times a day, dropping everything to take them shopping, or making sure every vacation and family outing includes them. Making a decision on their own becomes unthinkable; acting on their own becomes unforgivable.

Naturally, there will be times when legitimate health concerns or life adjustments cause us to bind together and spend vast quantities of time or effort in helping a needy parent. As we mentioned earlier, trials like these *build* positive, valuing lines of loyalty between parent and child. It's only when the "illness" or demands on a child come from contrived sicknesses or unquenchable, selfish needs of a problem parent that this second dishonoring home lowers a child's worth.[5]

If you grew up in a home with imprisoning obligations, you don't need any further explanations. You've already felt the twisting and tightening of these bonds and the gripping prison they can become. If you haven't been raised in such a home, you should be thankful. Also be aware that in your own home, laying down imprisoning obligations has the possibility of greatly dishonoring a child for years to come.

The family scapegoat and the prisoner of unyielding obligations can develop incredibly strong negative attachments to the past and to parents. Before we look at how to break such hurtful bonds, we need to examine three other homes that can produce strong negative loyalty bonds.

CHAPTER SIXTEEN

Understanding the Dark Side of Family Loyalties: Part 2

Imagine standing with your arms stretched out and two of the biggest members of the Dallas Cowboys football team trying to pull you in opposite directions! That's how many children feel who get pulled in two different directions by their parents. It also represents a third home in which negative loyalty bonds wrap around a child. Children who are *caught in the middle of a parental power struggle* have a hard time escaping from these patterns to move on to more healthy ways of life.

3. CAUGHT IN THE MIDDLE

Jim felt this way. From the time he was born until his parents finally divorced, they fought battle after battle. For a number of years, Jim was such a joy to them that they kept their eyes off their problems with each other and focused most of their attention on him. And talk about attention! Even though an only child does tend to get more time with his parents, Jim was off the charts when it came to being smothered with affection. The only problem came when his parents decided to divorce, and twelve-year-old Jim was expected to choose sides.

All the love and attention Jim had received built a deep

love and loyalty for both parents. You can imagine his confusion at being asked to sever relationships with one parent if he wanted to maintain the acceptance of the other. As charges and countercharges were fought out between his parents at home and in court, Jim didn't know where to turn. And neither do many other children who get caught in the middle. A child like Sharon, for example.

Sharon's mother was always open to new things. Unfortunately, that led her to accept the teachings of a cult that's popular today. As a teen-ager, Sharon was torn between staying in her father's church or embracing her mother's newfound religion. Choosing one path meant rejecting the other; not choosing at all still left her out in the cold. After agonizing days, Sharon decided to remain with her father in her home church. In turn, her mother bristled with anger and cut off contact with Sharon until she, too, became "enlightened."

Putting children in the position of having to make choices like saying yes to one parent and no to the other brings to light negative bonds of loyalty. All too often, parents pull on these lines, trying to move their children over to their side of an argument.

In the Scriptures, Jonathan must have felt pulled in this way in his intimate friendship with David. Protect David, and go against his father. If he sided with his father, he might see his best friend killed. In fact, Jonathan's father, Saul, became so angry when he sensed his son was more loyal to David that he hurled his spear at David and tried to pin him to the wall! (See 1 Samuel 19:1–10.)

Putting a child in the middle of a power struggle is unfair, and it also lowers his sense of self-worth. Parents who truly want to raise the value of their children will keep from making their children's loyalty a tool for defending their own position.

4. ALL GROWN UP . . . AND STILL A CHILD

Did you ever sneak into the attic or basement and try on some of your father's or mother's clothes when you were young? Most of us enjoyed dressing up like "Mom or Dad." It made us feel special and "just like them." There's a kind of home where the play-acting becomes real and a child is forced to take over as the parent in the household. Basically, the child is told, "Pass over childhood and go directly to adulthood." When she does, negative lines of loyalty can pull her away from developing into the person she could be. This happened to Martha.

Martha's mother was an alcoholic. It made little difference that Martha was only nine years old when her mother's drinking began to incapacitate her. For several years she had already been "mother" to her poor little sisters and brothers.

Because of her mother's irresponsibility and inability to care for the children, parental responsibilities fell on Martha's shoulders. Martha, not her mother, would take care of the cooking, cleaning, and doing the laundry. She would sneak into the living room when her mother had passed out and steal money from her purse so she and the little ones could eat.

Years went by, and Martha learned how to be a mother. However, she never had the chance to learn how to be a child and how to let someone else take some responsibility. Forced to become a parent to her brothers and sisters, she developed extremely deep bonds of loyalty to them.

There's nothing wrong with close ties between siblings, of course. Martha and her brothers and sisters have a special closeness because of all they suffered together. But Martha developed intense lines of loyalty that shifted to the darker side. Like many "parentified" children, she continued to feel incredibly responsible for her siblings long after they were grown up, and she failed to develop as a person because of it.

At age thirty-nine, Martha still carries on the role of the parent in her home, only now her "baby" is her mother. Martha's brothers and sisters never discussed who would take care of Mother when she got older or the alcohol made her too confused and disabled to live alone. They simply assumed that Martha would be the one to do so. After all, Martha had always been the one to "take care of people and things" in the family. "She must enjoy it," they concluded.

Martha has never married, and she constantly checks on her brothers and sisters and their families. Although they're always glad to see her, they grow tired of her need to be so closely involved in the intimate details of their lives. But negative lines of loyalty keep Martha duty bound to play out a role she should never have been given.

For a number of children, being in a single-parent home or a home where they are forced to grow up fast can build a certain strength and character into them. However, saddle children with the responsibility of being full-time parents when they should be full-time children, and watch the problems begin and their self-worth drop.

5. CHOOSE YOU THIS DAY

The fifth type of home that lowers the worth of children demands perhaps the greatest loyalty from them and offers the least in return. It's a home where children are expected to choose their parents' way over and above God's way. Sometimes this kind of negative loyalty becomes only too clear when children seek to replace it. That's exactly what Mark found to be true with his family.

Mark came from a family that truly was a dynasty. His grandfather had followed two simple principles for making money. The first was to find out where people were going and get there first. He had done this by purchasing several farms in what was once a sleepy valley in southern California, and his foresight had netted him millions.

The second principle was to "do unto others before they do you in." Mark's grandfather and his father based their business on cutthroat corporate politics. Stand in their way on a business deal, and get mowed down. Cheat if you could, but be sure you were so good at it that you wouldn't get caught. This also included cheating on income taxes and buying off zoning decisions whenever they could. Whatever it took to be "successful," the end justified the means.

With their own employees, Mark's father and grandfather made sure they kept a "professional distance" from even the most senior executives in the firm. Keeping everyone at arm's length made it easier to fire whomever they wanted whenever they wanted with the desired effect of putting the "fear of God" into the ones who remained.

Mark was the heir apparent to the family business. And as in many wealthy families, his childhood and adolescent life was a grooming time to prepare him for future responsibilities. Mark lived out his family script to perfection—right up until the end of high school, when he attended a church youth retreat and became a Christian.

As the only believer in the family, Mark began to question things that he had never questioned before. Why had that vice president been fired when he was only two years away from retirement? Why did his father have so many "secret" meetings when it was time to invest his personal and company profits? Why did he continue to get "that look" when he first met people who had worked with his father on a business deal?

Unlike his father, Mark developed an interest in things apart from the family business, particularly spiritual things. While he was at home, he became involved in the leadership of his church youth group. In college, he began a discipleship program with the Navigators, and within a year he was leading a group.

Both in the many comments he received from those he worked with and discipled and in his own heart, Mark felt called to the ministry. He talked at length with his pastor and spent hours in prayer by himself. With graduation only a year away, Mark made the decision to send in his application to seminary rather than law school.

When Mark spoke to his father about his change in plans, he found out about family loyalties in a hurry. With all the commotion he caused, Mark felt branded and disloyal. Invisible obligations and expectations that had been hiding in the shadows suddenly came to light and swirled around him. Whether it was a disturbing card from his mother or his uncle flying out from Boston to try to "talk some sense" into him, doing what had once seemed so right now became a family battlefield.

In the book of Matthew, Jesus made several strong statements about discipleship: "Do not think that I came to bring peace on earth. . . . For I have come to 'set a man against his father, a daughter against her mother, and a daughter-in-law against her mother-in-law' " (Matthew 10:34–35). Particularly in homes where negative lines of loyalty pull a child away from a relationship with Christ, Jesus brings a sword to cut these lines, not peace to compromise with them. Yet such statements are hard to accept.

Trying to discern the Lord's will in the midst of such family pressure was the most difficult and confusing thing Mark had ever done. After several months of intense pressure from home, he gave up trying to understand what God might be telling him. Regardless of what God's best might be, Mark refused to question a strongly held family pattern. Instead of maintaining his convictions despite the cost, he slowly broke his ties with the Navigators and pulled away from his church.

All-Too-Common Choices

Before you pick up stones to hurl at Mark, take a long look at your own life. Does your lack of spiritual growth keep you in step with how your parents viewed spiritual things? Is that uncontrolled temper you struggle with a reflection of something you once saw in your father? Can that tendency to overspend, even when it puts a strain on your marriage, call to mind patterns you've seen in the past? Does that tendency to fudge a little—when you should be totally honest—trace its roots to what you saw in your parents? Could your discomfort with being warm and huggy with your children, even when you know they need it, stem from your missing out on being touched?

Your relationship with your parents can leave many positive marks on your life, but there can also be strong negative lines of loyalty. And if you're to be free to build love and value into your children or to see it in your own life, you must recognize these factors.

Today, Mark's marriage is in trouble, and he struggles in his relationship with his sons. And Mark, not his father, is the one the government is investigating for improper business dealings. In the midst of counseling, Mark traces the incredible hostility, guilt, and shame he carries inside and his struggles in his spiritual life back to one primary factor. His life has been controlled by unbending negative family loyalties.

In many homes, the choice to honor God or give precedence to unbiblical family rules is put squarely on the table. Such homes reverberate with statements like these: "Who cares about the problems it causes, in *this* home the *men* in the family drink!" "Pay no attention to your wife's (or husband's) need to spend time with her family. There are too many important family gatherings on our side of the family to spend time with them. And besides, we have to think about what's best for the children—and you know who can buy them the nicest presents." In other homes, the choice is more subtly placed on the table, yet it's every bit as prevalent.

Some families automatically turn their back on the one who picks up the card marked "Live Life God's Way." Try to explain to some parents or family members why being a Christian can bring about changes in lifestyle, and the chasm between the two sides opens wider.

Up to this point, we've tried to illustrate five homes that tend to wrap strong lines of loyalty around children and pull them back from becoming all they could be. These five homes dishonor children rather than build honor into their lives. Is there a way to break free from these negative loyalties and replace them with the positive one we looked at previously?

For each of the people we used as an illustration, the answer is yes. Each of them went through the difficult process of identifying negative loyalties in their lives and replacing them with lifelines of security and support.

TURNING FAMILY WRONGS AROUND

Why is it so hard to turn family wrongs around and so easy to repeat a past pattern? As we've looked in the Scriptures and talked with couples and families across the country, we've found at least three things that often interact and keep people in bondage, leading them to repeat the past.

1. Bondage Can Feel So Familiar.

For many people, even for the nation of Israel, negative experiences lay down strong lines of negative loyalty. Not only that, but the fear of giving up familiar bonds is greater than the faith a person has to have when he's free.

For hundreds of years before Moses led God's people out of Egypt, the nation had suffered in captivity. Just give them a taste of freedom, and watch how appreciative they would be, right? Wrong! Three days after Moses miraculously parted the Red Sea, the people began to complain that the only water they had to drink was bitter (See Exodus 15:23–24.) (as if the God who parted the sea couldn't supply a glass of water when they needed it). A few days later, the people said to Moses, "Oh, that we had died by the hand of the LORD in the land of Egypt, whe we sat by the pots of meat and when we ate bread to the full! For you have brought us out into this wilderness to kill this whole assembly with hunger" (Exodus 16:3).

Just a few weeks out of slavery, and already Egypt wasn't looking so bad. Almost overnight, negative lines of loyalty began their pull to bring Israel back into bondage. Even when God supplied manna for them to eat, they complained again, saying, "We remember the fish which we ate freely in Egypt, the cucumbers, the melons, the leeks, the onions, and the garlic; but now our whole being is dried up; there is nothing at all except this manna" (Numbers 11:5–6). For some reason, bondage can look different once we are free. We may have cried and groaned under our burden, but when we leave our familiar cell, it may not look so bad.

Perhaps each of us has experienced something similar to

what the Israelites felt. Did you ever have a dating relationship where there were problems galore and very few positive things to commend it? On the night you broke up with that person, do you remember saying, "Boy, what did I ever see in him (or her)?" A few weeks or months later, however, do you remember looking back and saying to yourself, "Maybe that dating relationship really wasn't so bad after all. I wonder if we should get back together?"

Ever since the Garden of Eden, men and women have had a tendency to lean back into bondage and fear going down a new path on their own. We may be miserable in our present situations, but at least it's a familiar misery. Our shoes may be filled with holes and unable to keep out the cold, but "My, are they comfortable."

It takes courage to work at freeing ourselves from past patterns. It takes courage to look honestly at our parents and how they raised us. It takes courage to admit past mistakes and to confront wrong in the family without dishonoring our parents or siblings in the process. It takes only complacency to remain where we are.[1]

2. Fear = Procrastination.

Why do so many people put off confronting wrongs or making long overdue changes? A second reason is that just like the Roman governor Felix, they become afraid of change and let that fear keep conviction at arm's length.

Felix was a Roman ruler who lived an immoral life. At one point, he had his brother killed so he could marry his sister-in-law.[2] But Felix is best known for being one of the world's great procrastinators. He had the opportunity to have the apostle Paul point out areas he needed to change in his life, yet fear closed the door to genuine change, and procrastination sneaked in the window and made itself at home. "Felix . . . sent for Paul and heard him concerning the faith in Christ. Now as he reasoned about righteousness, self-control, and the judgment to come, Felix was afraid and answered, 'Go away for now; when I have a convenient time I will call for you'" (Acts 24:24–25).

Perhaps there's been something that convicted you in

reading the Scriptures, this book, or another Christian book. Some of you may have realized for the first time that your life is being held in check by negative lines of loyalty. You may have seen yourself in one of the homes we illustrated, and you may not have had the courage to confront your past or stop dishonoring your parents. Perhaps you've seen something you've done with your children that lowers their self-worth and ties them up in knots, yet you put off changing your behavior. What can head off any attempt at needed change? *Fear*.

Jim really wanted to talk to his father about problems in the past, but he was afraid of the reaction he would get. Martha knew that she shouldn't yell at her brothers and sisters, but facing that problem in her life might make her face others as well, and she was afraid of what she would find. Gretta was tired of being the scapegoat in her family, but fear kept her from bringing her hurt out into the open. It's never easy to go through the process of uncovering negative lines of loyalty. It goes against our very make-up.

Painful Memories. An interesting study conducted a few years ago sought to understand how the brain stores memories of past events. Through electrical stimulation, the researchers activated certain areas of the brain that they thought might "hold" memories. To their delight, many experimental subjects recalled memories with striking clarity, even if the events had occurred years earlier. As the experiment progressed, however, an unexpected side effect developed. When the subjects recalled a particular event, they also experienced many of the feelings associated with the memory. So painful were some of the feelings that several of the experimental subjects refused to continue with the research.[3]

Many people fear bringing up the past because their memories bring back feelings that are too painful. Yet only when negative patterns and lines of loyalty are revealed and dealt with honestly can they lose their powerful effect.

3. More of the Same Doesn't Bring Change.

Some of you may have difficulty breaking negative lines of loyalty because you've grown too accustomed to the pain or because fear of change rears its head and you put things on hold—again. Although these are two frequent reasons for not following through with needed changes, many people repeat a past hurtful pattern because deep inside they think it will go away on its own. They know there must be happiness in there somewhere, and it will come one day if they continue to do things the "old-fashioned way." Even if they've spent a lifetime casting into the same spot and never catching a fish, that trophy catch must be in there somewhere.

Imagine watching someone sitting in front of a television set, anxiously waiting for the programs to begin. He's been waiting for days to catch a glimpse of the shows. But as you look over to the set he's staring at, you notice there's no picture. The set isn't even plugged in to an electrical outlet!

When you mention this to the person, he replies, "Don't bother me with that. I was watching this television one time, and it worked perfectly. I'm sure it's just warming up."

How does this relate to people who put off change in their lives? There is a principle we see very often in counseling that many people put into practice in their homes: people are convinced that *more of the same will eventually bring change*. Many people want change, but they don't want to do anything to bring it about. Like the man who waited anxiously for the television set to go on, they feel that just wanting and waiting to change will eventually bring needed changes to life.

Challenging a person to change his behavior makes great motivational sense. Unquestionably, that's why many spiritual life and marriage seminars exist. People pay top dollar to get motivated to change, but rarely is there any accountability following the cheerleading session, and few needed changes take place. (That's a major reason why we stress small group follow-up so much if you attend any of our seminars.)

The fact is that *more of the same does not bring change*.

If you sit tight and let a parent manipulate you, the negative bonds can continue to hurt your parent and you for a lifetime.[4]

The tremendous pastor of our home church is Darryl DelHousaye, and he frequently issues us this challenge in his sermons: "Scripturally, the stronger person always initiates the peace." You need to be the strong one in dealing with problems. Not doing so is like having a broken watch and waiting for it to repair itself. It can keep you operating on the wrong time for years.

If you're motivated to change and are willing to give up the familiarity of your bonds and the fear of doing something new, how can you begin to change? By making sure you're plugged in to the Source of Life where you can receive the inner power you need to change even the most destructive patterns from the past.

KNOWING WHAT TO PLUG IN TO AND WHEN WE'RE UNPLUGGED

Let's go back to an example we used in the previous chapter. While we'll be using this one woman's story to illustrate our points, what we told her is also what we explained to each person whose story we mentioned in this chapter.

Gretta was the young woman who suffered terribly as the scapegoat of her family. She was hated by her mother and rejected by her brothers and sisters. She wanted to change things in her home, and later in her own life and family as well. She would cry herself to sleep at times, wanting so much for things to change. How could she possibly deal with all the hurts she experienced and break free of the negative bonds that held her?

As we began counseling with Gretta, we discovered that in many ways, her desires in life were the same as anyone else's. She longed for others to highly value her. She wanted inner happiness, calm, and contentment. Yet because of her negative home situation, she received only anger, bitterness, and defeat.

It was as if Gretta's life were a lamp with a single cord. She wanted desperately to see her life lit up with positive feelings and a warm inner calm. She wanted the joy of knowing she was accepted unconditionally by her mother and loved by her brothers and sisters. Yet every time she tried plugging her life in to her natural family, the bulb remained dark, or even worse, she received terrible shocks.

Do you know what can happen when something that should reward you turns around and shocks you? For some people, it can cause enough despair to lead to suicide.

Pushing a Painful Lever

Years ago, there was a classic study done on some mice who were each placed in an experimental box.[5] On one end of the box was a bar that would drop a food pellet when it was pressed. Being curious and active little animals, these mice weren't in their boxes very long before they accidentally pushed or stood on the bars and a food pellet came out. It didn't take very long after that before the mice were pressing their bars like crazy whenever they were in the mood for food.

But then the researchers did something to the metal bar in each box. They attached wires to each bar that were connected at the other end to a large battery. Every time a mouse touched his bar, he would receive a terrible shock along with a pellet of food.

Smarting and confused, the mice would usually push the bar a second time and sometimes a third, each time receiving the painful shock. What do you think happened after that? Even when their hunger threatened their lives, most of them would die in the box, unwilling to be shocked again. And did you know the really tragic thing about this study? After the third shock, the researchers had turned off the battery. There was no longer a shock when the mouse pressed the bar! He could have pressed it and received all the food he needed, but he wouldn't face the potential pain of pushing it again.

Over the years, Gretta had been shocked so many times by her family that she also felt like giving up. The very people who should have given her love and acceptance had given her only pain and hurt, and she thought seriously about taking her own life.

Gretta didn't attempt suicide, but she was so tired of darkness and being shocked, and so desirous of light in her life, that she tried plugging in to anything that she thought might bring her power and warmth. She tried lighting her life by plugging it in to friends, dating, school, jobs, houses, even drugs and alcohol. And every time she plugged in to any of those sources, they, too, left her trapped in darkness and afraid she would never see the light she longed for.

Do you know someone like Gretta? Has a dishonoring home left that person searching for the light of love and peace and full of the darkness of fear and despair? We hope he or she can discover what Gretta did. There is really only one place where any of us can plug in to find the satisfaction in life we so desperately need.

Plugging in to the Source of Life

When Gretta finally discovered that she needed to plug in to the Source of Life, Jesus Christ, for the first time she saw her life light up. In His love she found unconditional acceptance (Romans 8:38–39; John 10:1ff.; Hebrews 13:5). In His power she found the strength to be joyful in spite of her circumstances (Philippians 4:11–14; 1 Peter 1:6–9). In His hand she found a spiritual family at a church that loved her unconditionally, and from Him she received the peace she had never before found (John 14:6; 1 John 5:1ff.).

Perhaps you need to consider what your life is plugged in to. Many people try to carry around dozens of cords and plug them in to the Lord and many other things, but God has designed us with one cord and only one place where we can plug in and find lasting life and power—Himself.

Gretta left our office one afternoon after making the most significant decision anyone can make. For the first time, she plugged her life in to the Source of Life. For the next year and a half, Gretta made a daily decision to look only to the Lord to light up her life. As we mentioned earlier, it takes thirty days of doing something consistently before it

208

becomes a habit. Gretta didn't give up, and soon she found that the first thing she did in the morning and the last thing she did at night was to say to herself, "Time to plug in to what God says about me and unplug from the disappointing sources I'm plugged in to, to bring light into my life!"

Whenever she found herself angry with her husband or impatient with her children, she took time to realize that she was really plugged in to them, trying to use them for fulfillment, and they were frustrating or shocking her. Most important, whenever she thought back to her family background and her light began to dim, she would unplug her worth from the past and plug it in to what her heavenly Father had to say about her.

This concept is so important that I (Gary) have taken an entire book titled *Joy That Lasts*[6] to talk about it. If you're struggling through problems or a past like one of the homes we've pictured, we would encourage you to take things a step further and practice plugging in to a personal relationship with God and unplugging from unfulfilling expectations placed on people or things.

Persisting to the End

For Gretta, it took a year and a half of consistently making the decision to plug in to God and unplug from others before she began to feel released from her past hurts. But that's not the end of the story.

At fifty-one years of age, Gretta began calling her eighty-six-year-old mother and telling her for the first time in years that she loved her. Because she was no longer dependent on her mother to light up her life, she was free to love without any expectations. The result was that she began to feel compassion for her mother instead of hate, and she discovered things she had never known about her mother's past. For one thing, she was shocked to discover that her mother had come from a home where there was almost constant sexual abuse. Instead of dishonoring her mother (and lowering her own worth as a result), Gretta made a decision to honor and value her.

"No wonder she was never able to love me," Gretta told

us after discovering her mother's past. And with that admission, years of hurt and darkness began to be replaced by a love for the Lord, for her family, and even for herself that she had never known before. When God lights up our lives and fills us with love, it's a gift we can share freely with others, not the artificial light that comes only when people "earn" our love.

All the people we mentioned in this chapter and the last—Wayne with his imprisoning obligations, Jim with the way he was pulled to love one parent and not the other, Mark whose family loyalties cut him off from serving the Lord, and Gretta—first confronted their reasons for not changing and then began plugging in to the Source of Life. When their lives were lit up by being consistently plugged in to Christ, they were able to see the negative lines of loyalty that had held them down for so long. Then they had the freedom to receive God's love and the inner power to deal with the effects of their past.

While it didn't happen overnight and they also had to learn to find value in their trials,[7] they are freer today than they've been in years. Their freedom comes from being plugged in to the only permanent source of love, joy, and peace.

The six aspects of honor we've discussed so far have the potential to make lasting, positive changes in our children's self-worth—that is, if the seventh aspect of honor is laid on top of all the others. In this final aspect, we go to the power source we need to balance and blend each element together and see it make a lasting change in our own lives.

CHAPTER SEVENTEEN

Offering Honor to God

Every day, parents are in the process of teaching their children to honor or dishonor God, even if they never use religious words. That was certainly the case in Don's home. His parents thought that part of being educated included a healthy dose of skepticism and the intellectual questions about a "Supreme Being" that were taught at upper crust schools.

Don's parents were never very interested in formal religion, and they often criticized "religious fanatics" who believed in God and the Bible. After all, as his father would often say, "We Spencers are successful without having to rely on emotional crutches."

If the truth be known, Don's parents were never very interested in *anything* they couldn't put in their bank account or flaunt at the club, including Don. How did Don know this? By the hours of consistent time Mom and Dad devoted to gaining wealth and prestige, and the minutes of inconsistent time they spent trying to teach him he was valuable to them.

There was always another land deal his father had to save or another Junior League function his mom had to attend that kept them from meeting the lonely boy's deepest needs. It wasn't that Don didn't have inner longings or questions about God. Like most children, he sensed there was a Creator and Lord of creation by looking at nature (Romans

1:20) and by talking with several of his friends who came from Christian homes.

As the years went by, Don developed a thirst for God apart from any encouragement from his parents. The only problem stemmed from where he chose to quench that thirst. Like many boys and girls who grow up with a deep longing for God but are stiff-armed in approaching Him by their parents, Don was so parched and dry that he was willing to drink at any well, even one filled with poisoned water.

At age seventeen, Don became deeply entrenched in a nationwide cult that preaches family, love, and acceptance yet demands bondage and unquestioning allegiance. While it may not sound like much of a bargain, Don was eager to forfeit his parents and his future to join such a cult. After all, he told us, *it was the first place where he felt truly valuable to someone*.

Like Don's parents, many moms and dads are simply not aware of the powerful influence they have on their children's spiritual lives. Yet for those who want to have a positive spiritual impact on their children, we're excited to illustrate how the concepts we've been talking about throughout this book can become avenues for your children to raise their value of God.

LEADING CHILDREN TO THE SOURCE OF HONOR

For several chapters we've looked at how on a horizontal level, we can and should provide honor to our loved ones. However, for us to be able to love and value others as we should—and to teach them to do so—we must begin by making sure our vertical relationship with God is growing and developing.

The Lord is the source of honor, the One from whom it flows. Plugging into Him provides us with the power source we need to love our children or others. In fact, we are capable of loving others because we are first loved by Him (1 John 4:10–11, 19, 21). We have the power to treat others as valuable treasures because He treats us that way (Ephesians 1:18–19). We have a model for giving our loved ones a special position in our lives because of the place of honor we're allowed to share in His family (1 John 3:1).

Not only do the Scriptures give us principles and guidelines for motivating our children to honor God and others, but they also give us real life models we can follow.

Children love stories, and the Bible is full of examples of men and women who honored their relationship with God as their most priceless treasure and because they did, honored their loved ones. We can share with our children stories of people like Ruth, who honored her mother-in-law and stayed with her in her time of need (even when she could have legally abandoned her mother). (See Ruth 1:1ff.) The Old Testament saints who honored their children by providing a special blessing for them (Genesis 49:1ff.), or even James and later each of the disciples made the ultimate sacrifice to put their faith in the Lord before their very lives.

However, of all the great examples of faith, the ultimate example of someone who gave high value to people—even to those who did not deserve His attention—is our Lord Himself. He gives us the motivation to serve and honor others.

Traveling through a crowded city street, He stopped to call down an insignificant Zaccheus from a tree and confront a woman with a hemorrhage, who reached out in faith to touch Him for healing. Before the Last Supper, Jesus laid aside His position of honor at the Passover meal to wash the disciples' feet. I (Gary) have experienced someone washing my feet only once, but it was one of the most humbling and honoring experiences of my life.

At the cross, Christ honored His mother by placing her in the care of His beloved friend, He took the time to meet the dying request of a common criminal, and He even prayed for the forgiveness of those who nailed Him to the tree.

Because our heavenly Father made the decision to honor us—to count us of great value—through His Son's death on the cross, He opened wide the door for us to experience eternal life. On our own, none of us merits that life, nor

God's grace or favor, but on the basis of Christ's sacrifice, we are no longer enemies but actually beloved friends. C. S. Lewis once put it this way:

> To please God . . . to be a real ingredient in the divine happiness . . . to be loved by God, not merely pitied, but delighted in as an artist delights in his work or a father in a son—it seems impossible, a weight or burden of glory which our thoughts can hardly sustain. But so it is.[1]

Each of the major sections of this book speak specifically about honoring our children or loved ones, but each can also apply to our learning to honor God.

- **We obey His word, gaining life and making our days pleasant by giving honor to our parents (Deuteronomy 17:6).**
- **When we acknowledge God has a special plan for our lives, even in the midst of trials, we honor Him and learn to depend on Him as our source of life.**
- **Understanding our strengths as parents can make us better vessels to serve our children and others.**
- **Like the disciples of old, we, too, can find a helpful balance between nestling close to Him (belonging) and going out to serve others (separateness).**
- **Spending time in God's Word can alert us to the boundaries He has put up around things and people that should or should not enter our lives.**
- **Looking to His loyal-love as a model, we have the basis for building positive loyalties into our own and our children's lives.**

Each aspect of honor needs to be filtered through our relationship with the Lord and can be used to draw us closer to Him. By understanding and applying the three major aspects of the definition of honor, we can see our children's spiritual lives blossom and develop.

DRAWING GOLD FROM THE DEFINITION
OF HONOR

A picture is indeed worth a thousand words for teaching children lessons in right living. That's true of the three word pictures we can use with our children to illustrate what it means for them (or us) to dishonor or honor God.

1. Learning a "Weighty" Lesson on Dishonoring Others

As we saw in chapter 2, the word picture behind *dishonor* is a "vapor" or "steam." How can a word picture like this help a child understand a concept like dishonoring someone? One creative parent used it to illustrate to her daughter what it meant to dishonor God's Word by hurting a friend.

Jammie was a nine-year-old who was already quite a people pleaser. That's why she was swayed so much by her friends' opinions on who to invite to her slumber party. Jammie had a cousin her age who lived nearby. The girls were the same age and for years had been close friends and playmates. However, in the last few years they had drifted apart. Jammie was attractive and was becoming popular at school, while her cousin had long struggled with a weight problem and was not well liked by others.

Jammie mentioned to her friends at school that she was going to invite her cousin. "No," they said emphatically, "she's too fat and ugly!" Rather than stand her ground and defend her cousin or insist she be a part of the party, Jammie joined in with their giggles and decided not to invite her after all.

When Jammie's mother asked her if she was going to invite her cousin, Jammie tried to change the subject and ignore the question. Finally she lied and said her cousin was "busy" and couldn't attend. After the party, however, quite by accident, Jammie's mother found out her niece had not been busy and was deeply hurt at being overlooked by her former best friend.

As a Christian parent, Jammie's mother was concerned

about her daughter's actions. As a wise mother as well, she used the experience to teach her daughter the difference between honoring and dishonoring words and actions. Having learned the literal meaning behind dishonoring someone, she decided to demonstrate it to her daughter in a creative and convicting way.

That winter evening, when it was time for Jammie's bath, her mother went in with her and took along an extremely heavy paperweight from the study. "Jammie, do you know what it means to dishonor someone?" she asked. When Jammie said she really didn't know, her mother told her to try to grab hold of the steam that was coming out of the faucet as they filled the tub with warm water.

"How much do you think that steam weighs, Jammie?" her mother asked.

"Not very much!" her daughter said with a giggle as she tried to grab handfuls of steam from the air.

Then handing Jammie the paperweight, her mother asked, "How much do you think this weighs?"

"Tons!" said Jammie as she struggled to hold up the paperweight with both hands.

Then her mother explained that what she had just illustrated was like what Jammie had done to her cousin. "Jammie, when you dishonor someone, you treat her like a vapor, like she's only as heavy as that steam coming up from the tub. But when you honor someone, you treat her as if she's important and carries a lot of weight like Dad's paperweight.

"Honey, did you realize that by not inviting your cousin to your slumber party, and by lying to me, you treated both of us as though we had as little weight as the steam you tried to catch? Not only that, but God's Word also tells us we're to love those who may not be so lovable, and especially that we're not to lie. When you hurt your cousin and lied to me, you also treated God as if He didn't weigh anything either. Is that what you wanted to do by your actions?"

As her mother's words dawned on her, Jammie's smile turned into tears of conviction. For the first time she understood how her dishonoring actions had affected her cousin and her mother and had even dishonored God. After a good cry during her bath, Jammie asked her mom to forgive her, and she prayed and asked God to forgive her, also. Perhaps hardest of all, she then went into the kitchen, called her cousin, and asked to be forgiven.

In the Scriptures we read, "You who make your boast in the law, do you dishonor God through breaking the law?"[2] Like Jammie, when we disobey God's Word and treat it like a vapor, we dishonor Him. The lower our value of the Scriptures, the easier it will be for us to treat His rock-solid words as sifting sand and brush them aside whenever it's convenient to do so.

2. Going in Search of a Priceless Treasure

As we're sure you remember, one word picture behind the concept of honor is to view someone as a special treasure, and another is to give him a highly respected position in our lives. When we use these analogies, the door is wide open to teaching our children practical lessons in loving God.

At the time we're writing this chapter, stores are gearing up for the mobs of people who will be looking for bargains between Thanksgiving and Christmas. To use this analogy of shopping, if our lives were like a department store, what price would we put on the Lord?

Chuck Swindoll has an exceptional book of layman's theology that we highly recommend, *Growing Deep in the Seasons of Life*.[3] In it is a convicting chapter titled "Mary's Little Lamb." At the close of that chapter, he tells the story of a major department store chain that had a cuddly, washable, plastic "baby Jesus" for sale. It came complete with artificial straw and was distributed to all their stores nationwide. The dolls, however, proved to be a sales flop. One store manager became worried at the backlog of "Jesus" dolls and had a sign made up: "JESUS, MARKED DOWN 50%. GET HIM WHILE YOU CAN!"

What a beautiful description of the way the people of the world look at our Lord! They put Him in plastic; they mark

Him down; they try to manipulate Him to gain riches (as Felix and others in the Scriptures have done for centuries).[4]

However, putting the story of this doll aside, what kind of price tag would you put on Jesus in your home? Do your actions and attitudes toward Him convey that He's on discount special and not of great value in your life?

Let Them Catch Your Passion. The best way to convey to children that the Lord is of great value is to illustrate it by the way you live. Children are God's little spies. They know what you treasure without your telling them. You may tell them they're important, but if you can't take your eyes off the TV set long enough to make eye contact with them when they're talking to you, they know what's more valuable to you. You may tell them your relationship with Christ is first in your life, yet you say grace at meals only when company comes or consistently skip church to watch the game. Your value system is showing, and you can be sure that they're watching.

The best way to teach children to value God, then, is to develop a passion for knowing Him. For parents who may be struggling in this area (and most of us do at times), we recommend two exceptional books that can help them get back into God's Word and into valuing God and others.[5] For parents who are already doing a good job of attaching high value to God, we have a practical suggestion to help children learn to count the Lord as a special treasure.

It's one thing to take an element that's already beautiful, like gold, and shape a precious ring or necklace out of it. It's quite another thing, however, to take something that appears worthless and bring beauty and value out of *it*. Throughout the Scriptures, there are examples of humble people and things that God has taken and transformed into valuable creations. That's what one father tried to communicate to his children.

Recently, the children had lost their only remaining grandparent, and their father wanted to be sure they understood what a loving, powerful God they had even in the midst of their loss. This was important because one son in particular was having a very difficult time "liking" God and attaching any value to Him after the loss of his grandmother (the same way adults often react to a loss).

As we've already mentioned, seeing God's presence and the value that can be gained in trials is a tremendous way for children to continue to attach value to God. However, spinning off the definition of honor he had learned, this father wanted to give them a living example of how God could take tragedy and turn it into triumph. So on a Saturday morning, he gathered the children together and had each of them plant a sweet pea seed in his or her own little container of potting soil. While they were all having fun planting and watering, he explained to them what the Scriptures say about the resurrection of the dead, that our bodies are "sown in dishonor" and "raised in glory" (1 Corinthians 15:43).

He told them that the seeds they were planting would die, but that one day soon they would bring forth fruit or a flower—and the same thing would be true for their grandmother. Her physical body had died and been placed in the ground, but one day God will raise it up, imperishable, in a new and beautiful form as glorious as any flower.

As he explained this to the children, the son who was struggling seemed to let the words bounce off him, and he remained angry and sullen—until the first sprouts of green shot up from his planting. That's when the truth of his father's words sank in. Instead of continuing to be angry with God because he lost his grandmother, he had a new reason and hope for what had scared him the most about the funeral—watching his grandmother's casket being lowered into the ground.

Having a picture of a scriptural truth growing in front of him gave this young boy a new way to honor God by seeing His incredible power to bring life. Instead of "marking down" God's value in that home, a wise parent used a teachable moment to raise his children's value of God.

Growing seeds together isn't the only way to teach children about God's value in their lives. A parent could study with them what it means to say Jesus is our Good Shepherd or read them stories in the Scriptures that speak of His unchanging love for us (John 10:11–15; 15:9–10). Simply talking about the Cross can be a graphic way to illustrate to children how valuable they are to God, and it can raise their view of Jesus at the same time.

Thus far, we've looked at how children can see their value of God raised when they learn what it means to dishonor Him and how Jesus remains a priceless treasure even during times of trial. There's also a third aspect of the definition of honor that can give you some handles on teaching your children to highly value God.

3. Uncovering the Place of Honor (or Dishonor) God Plays in a Child's Life

There's one method you can use to evaluate the place God holds in your children's lives and raise it higher if need be. If your sons or daughters are in grade school or older, you can ask them what they consider to be the most valuable things in their lives. You may be surprised at the answers. Grant was when he asked his junior-high-aged son this question, yet it gave him a starting place to help his son raise his sense of value of God.

Grant's son had a real problem going to Sunday school and would skip it nine times out of ten. When Grant asked his son what was most important in his life, he found out that the boy's relationship with God was in sixth place— just behind television.

Grant could have reacted at this point, but instead he asked his son another question: "On a one to ten scale, with ten being of tremendous value to you—something you really treasure like that autographed poster in your room— where would you rate your sense of value for God?"

"About a four, I guess," answered his son.

Instead of getting angry and lecturing him, Grant asked, "Son, what would it take to move that four up higher toward a ten?"

Without a moment's hesitation, his son answered, "I always feel so stupid when I'm in Sunday school class. Everybody knows all the verses and where to find them, and I get embarrassed and hate it when they call on me."

Being embarrassed when you're a junior-higher is almost

the same as being disbarred if you're an attorney! His fear of the other children's finding out how little he knew of the Scriptures was at the heart of what was holding him back from going to class.

Grant met with his son each week and went through the verses and lessons the junior-high class was studying. After several months of consistently studying the Bible together, Grant's son was going regularly to the junior-high class, and Grant felt he had never been closer to his son than in the times they spent together studying God's Word.

Before we end our look at the concept of honor, we'd like to offer one final story that we feel captures the heart of much of what we've wanted to say. It's an example of the tremendous impact one family member can have on the rest of his family by putting what he learned about honor into action.

CHAPTER EIGHTEEN

Honoring Others in Action

We've explained and illustrated the biblical concept of honor and shown practical ways a parent can put this concept to work in his home. But when all is said and done, does it really work? Does honoring God, honoring others, and raising our own value in Him really cause the changes we've talked about in this book?

As we close our discussion of this life-changing concept, we'd like to share a beautiful story of a man who grew up feeling the brutal effects of being dishonored, but who excitedly told us of a miraculous change that took place in his life and his family's as he learned to honor God, himself, and others.

LIVING IN DISHONOR—CHOOSING
TO GIVE HONOR

Denny was the oldest of five children in an alcoholic home. As any child knows who grows up in such a home, there are all kinds of drinkers. Some become passive and sleep away their lives in a stupor. Others become violent and use the alcohol to rationalize their deep hostility. Unfortunately for Denny and his sisters, their father was a combination of the two. As long as their father was in his withdrawn mood, Denny and his sisters were safe. But when he sobered up just enough to regain his senses, his anger wouldn't be appeased until someone had been hurt.

For Denny's sisters, that hurt came in the form of physical and sexual abuse. For him, it came at the cost of repeated beatings and verbal assaults. Like a thief who doesn't care what he steals or from whom he steals it, this father stole five children's innocence and trust and replaced it with shattered lives and broken futures.

As the years went by, Denny and his sisters followed the script we've already seen a number of times in this book. Being made to feel valueless, they acted out their emptiness in ways that damaged themselves and others. Two of Denny's sisters became prostitutes, another a practicing lesbian. And what of Denny? As in Harry Chapin's powerful song "Cat's in the Cradle," Denny's life echoed the pain-wrapped words, "I'm gonna be like you, Dad. You know I'm gonna be like you."

By the time he was in high school, Denny was a borderline alcoholic. He hated school and fought with students and teachers alike, but he found a positive release in football—that is, if you can call his excuse for legitimized brutality positive.

Denny loved football not for the clean sport of it, but for the opportunity it gave him to see how far he could go in hitting below the belt. He mastered the cheap shot and gloated over the players he had "taken out" with a knee injury or blind-sided with an illegal block. If he hadn't been big like his father and so filled with anger at all of life, he probably would never have been as good an athlete as he was. However, much to his and his parents' surprise, he was offered a scholarship at a major out-of-state university.

When Denny left his home at eighteen, he never expected to go back. Luckily, his father was in a stupor the day he left; there was no way he wanted to see him. Not that Denny was afraid of him anymore. During his sophomore year in high school, he had become so big and strong through weightlifting and playing football that he was able to beat his father brutally one night when his dad tried to "get physical" with his mother. Never again had his father tried to lift a hand against him or his mother, but Denny often egged him on to try to get one more chance to pulverize him.

Denny's life seemed similar to Cinderella's life. On game nights in college, he felt on top of the world in his football uniform. But when the stadium lights dimmed, so did any value he had as a person. Then came the knee injury in his junior year that ended his college career and his pro aspirations, and Denny had nothing in life to live for or give him hope.

Denny had married his high-school sweetheart their third year in college, but when he realized his sports career was over, he began drinking heavily again. After six months of his abusive behavior, his wife left him and school to return home to her parents. At the end of his final semester of college, he received his diploma in physical education and the notice from his wife's lawyer that his divorce had gone through. Denny would go through one more marriage and five years of increasing alcoholism before he hit rock bottom—and found the one door through which he could get back on his feet.

An old-high-school teammate who had moved to the city where Denny lived was the only person to keep in touch with him on a regular basis. And this man's life had a peace and joy that came from knowing the Source of Life, Jesus Christ. For nearly six years, this friend had invited Denny to church and had shared his faith with him at a ball game or over breakfast. At life's lowest ebb, Denny broke down on an Easter Day and went to church with his friend for the first time. "After all," he rationalized, "it's the thing to do on Easter." The last time Denny had been in a church (besides his first wedding) was when he was required to attend church as a young boy to play on their softball team.

While it was the last thing he expected, that morning Denny heard the simple plan of salvation explained, and he gave what was left of his shattered life over to the Savior. Over the next several years, God did a number of miraculous things in Denny's life. The first and biggest step was his being convinced of his need to deal with his drinking problem. After many months of wrestling with the decision, he began attending a Christian chapter of AA (Alcoholics Anonymous).

Then the Lord brought a most special gift into Denny's life, a Christian widow who loved him in spite of all his imperfections and his terrible past. As the years went by, their marriage was blessed with several children whom he loved beyond his wildest expectations.

Once Denny had made the decision to honor God, to place Him as the highest value in his life, honoring others came as a second step. He had never given his former wives the honor due them, but now he spent time listening to his wife and working at being sensitive to her needs. Where once he had all the potential of building negative lines of loyalty into his children, now he worked hard at providing the elements that build positive loyalties.

For several years Denny worked hard at treasuring his wife and children and giving them a special place in his life. But there was still one aspect of honor he needed to face. He had never made contact with his father in all those years, and he knew one day he would have to deal with that issue. At age thirty-five, prompted by several men in a small group Bible study who encouraged him to try to make things right with his father, he called him for the first time in over fifteen years. Alone in his office, he picked up the phone and dialed his father's number. When his father answered, Denny said, "Dad, this is your son Denny. And I just wanted you to know that I love you." Before he could say any more, his father hung up.

When he was forty, Denny became convicted again of his need to try to set things right, and he called and began the conversation with the same words as before: "Dad, I love you." For the second time, his father hung up as soon as he heard his son's words.

Two years later, Denny was at a special week-long Christian conference as a guest of one of the businessmen he called on in his work. He met a young couple who seemed extremely warm and friendly. Although he rarely let down his guard, they seemed to be genuinely interested in his life. Before he realized it, he was sharing a little of his struggle with his father.

The next morning as he went down to breakfast, Denny saw the young couple in the lobby, only they looked so worn out and tired that he walked over to them to see what was wrong. "Nothing's wrong," the couple said. "It's just that we've been up all night praying for you, Denny. We really feel that your relationship with your father is still crippling your life, especially your relationship with your wife. We think you need to try to contact him one more time."

Denny was almost shaking as he went to find his wife, and the two of them went up to their hotel room. He got the operator to place the call, and his father picked up the phone. "Dad," he began, "I want you to know I love you." Without a moment's hesitation, his father hung up for the *third* time.

Denny was stunned. He didn't know whether to cry or to get angry. He sat on the bed in silence until his wife demanded that he call his father back, this time insisting that he not hang up. Grudgingly, Denny did what his wife requested, and he rang his father again. "Dad, don't hang up on me," he said. "I want you to know that I love you, and I want you to know why."

For the next twenty minutes or so, he explained to his father how much his own life had changed, and how he could forgive and honor his dad now because of all he had been forgiven. His father listened, mostly in silence, and at the end of the call he felt great about what he had said. He had no idea, however, what response to expect from his father.

Several months passed. One day his mother called him at the office. "Denny, you'd better get back here. I don't think your father has long to live," she said. Immediately, he made plane reservations and began working with his secretary to cancel his appointments for the next few days. Then his mother called back.

"Never mind about coming back," she said. "We can't find your father. He's disappeared!"

A few hours later, Denny found out where his father had gone. His mother called him back and told him, "Your father called me, and he has checked himself into an alcohol rehabilitation clinic. *He wanted me to tell you that he wants you to come out before he dies to talk to him about spiritual things, and he wants to be sober when you talk to him.''*

Denny did go back, and he had the overwhelming joy of leading his father to Christ. He went with his father to the house of one of his sisters who lived in the same city as their parents. Denny's sister took a dozen steps back when they showed up at her door. She let them inside, and as they sat together on the couch, her father asked her forgiveness and reached over and touched her on the shoulder. As soon as her father touched her, she doubled over into the fetal position and started screaming. She got up, ran out of the house, and screamed that he should never, ever come back.

A few days later, Denny's father received a letter from that daughter. Listen to a few lines from her letter:

Father, your coming to see me was an outrage! There is no way you can come and preach forgiveness to me after all the scars I bear from you. For years, you have been all I have thought about. My every word, each decision I have made.

You have been responsible for me becoming a prostitute. You are responsible for my marriage that broke up. You are the reason I have had an operation so I can never have children—I'm afraid of what I'd do to them. You ask me to forgive you? You are not to be forgiven. You are to be conquered. If it takes me the rest of my life, I'll bury your memory. Don't ever call or come to see me again.

In a few months, Denny's father died, but not before he was able to talk to each of the other children and ask for and receive their forgiveness. The one unforgiving daughter did come to the funeral; she told Denny she wouldn't have missed that day for anything in the world.

THE GIFT OF HONOR

We chose this story to end the book for several reasons. From the moment Denny told us his story, we felt it was a beautiful example of each principle of honor. When it came to someone feeling of as little value as a mist, Denny had been dishonored all his life. Yet when it came to demonstrating the power of God when we give the gift of honor, he also stood out like a light.

Denny made a decision to honor others, beginning with his relationship with God, and by doing so he found a heart and desire for His Word and the power to take the next step. Alcoholics Anonymous and his Christian friends at church gave him a basis for breaking with the past and setting up a strong family.

As he gave honor to his wife and children, they had more security and love than he ever dreamed of or felt as a child. And when he made the decision to give honor to his father, with all the pain and heartache involved, it was as though he found the last missing piece of his own self-worth. At long last, he was free from many fears from the past and able to be at peace in the present.

Of all the joy in Denny's story, we appreciate its reality the most. While his days are brighter now and filled with God's light, in his family is a sister who has made totally opposite choices based on her past. His sister's life has been controlled for years because she's made a decision out of her hurt to treat others with as little value as she herself received. She devalues God and explains away the changes in her father and in Denny's life. She dishonors her father's memory with a passion, and she remains in emotional and spiritual chains. Denny has already seen treasure after treasure from his trials in the past; his sister thinks he is mentally ill for even thinking such thoughts.

So, we've come to the fork in the road. It's been our joy to walk with you as we've all learned more about the concept of honor. But we can walk with you no further.

Real life begins when you close this book and look up into the eyes of your children, your spouse, your Lord, or even that parent far away whose face never disappears.

We know for a fact that God is worthy to receive "glory, and honor and power" (Revelation 4:11). We also know that because we are made in His image, we are called on to "honor all people" (1 Peter 2:17).

Our prayer for you is that you'll not take the easy road of forgetfulness and procrastination, but that you'll take the narrow, steeper path that leads to building value into your loved ones' lives. It is in that journey that you'll learn for yourself and be able to teach your children to truly honor God, self, and others.

Gary Smalley   John Trent

© Maxine Kingston. *The Woman Warrior.* New York: Knopf, 1976.

Notes

Chapter 1

1. J. S. Brown, "Responses and Reaction to Motivation," *Journal of Comparative Physiological Psychology* 41 (1978): 450–65.
2. While there are any number of good books in print on parenting, some of our favorites are Charles R. Swindoll, *You and Your Child* (Nashville: Thomas Nelson, 1977); James Dobson, *Hide or Seek* (New Jersey: Revell, 1974); Henry Brandt, *I Want To Enjoy My Children* (Grand Rapids: Zondervan, 1975); Paul Meier, *Christian Child-Rearing and Personality Development* (Grand Rapids: Baker, 1977); Gordon MacDonald, *The Effective Father* (Wheaton: Tyndale, 1977); and Richard Allen, *Common Sense Discipline* (Ft. Worth: Sweet Publishing, 1986).
3. Lloyd Wright, "Correlates of Reported Drinking Problems among Male and Female College Students," *Journal of Alcohol and Drug Education* 28, no. 3 (1983): 48.
4. Thomas Darwin, "Parental Influences of Adolescent Self-Esteem," *Journal of Early Adolescence* 4, no. 3 (1984): 259–74.
5. Jane B. Burka and Lenora M. Yuen, *Procrastination: Why You Do It, What to Do About It* (Reading, Mass.: Addison-Wesley, 1983). This is a secular book with secular conclusions, but we found its exploration into the reasons why we procrastinate interesting and helpful.
6. Maxine Kingston, *The Woman Warrior* (New York: Knopf, 1976).

7. Frank Minirth, Paul Meier, and Bill Brewer et al., *The Workaholic and His Family* (Grand Rapids: Baker, 1981).

8. Joanna Norrell, "Parent-Adolescent Interaction: Influences on Depression and Mood Cycles," *Dissertation Abstracts International* 45, no. 4-A (1984): 1067.

9. James Juggins, "Parents as Change Agents with Low Self-Concept Elementary School-Age Children," *Dissertation Abstracts International* 43, no. 1-B (1983): 3385.

10. Edward McCraye, "Childhood Family Antecedents of Dependency and Self-Criticism: Implications for Depression," *Journal of Abnormal Psychology* 93, no. 1 (1983): 3.

11. Steven Ambrose, "Cognitive-Behavioral Parent Training for Abusive and Neglectful Parents," *Dissertation Abstracts International* 44 (1985): 2544.

12. Kim Openshaw, "Parental Influences of Adolescent Self-Esteem," *Journal of Early Adolescence* 4, no. 3 (1984): 239–41.

13. J. R. Heiman, "A Psychophysiological Exploration of Sexual Arousal Patterns in Females and Males," *Psychophysiology* 14, no. 3 (1977): 2266–74.

14. Jeff Hollowell, "The Relationship Between Self-Concept of Academic Ability and Discrepancy in Perceived Feedback Regarding Achievement," *Dissertation Abstracts International* 45, no. 1-A (1985): 125.

15. J. B. Rotter, "Generalized Expectancies for Internal Vs. External Control of Reinforcement," *Psychological Monographs* 80 (1981): 609.

16. T. Dawler, "Susceptibility to Heart Disease and Social Structure," *Studies in Cardiovascular Disease* 30 (1982): 671–76.

17. W. H. Masters and V. E. Johnson, *Human Sexual Inadequacy* (Boston: Little, Brown & Co., 1970).

18. Sue Evans, "Failure to Thrive: A Study of 45 Children and Their Families," *Journal of the American Academy of Child Psychology* 11 (1982): 440–57.

19. Sheldon Robinson, "Attempted Suicide During Adolescence: Elements of Self-Concept and Identification with a Rejecting Parent," *Dissertation Abstracts International* 44, no. 11-B (1984): 3539.

20. Robert Pandia, "Psychosocial Correlates of Alcohol and Drug Use of Adolescent Students and Adolescents in Treatment," *Journal of Studies on Alcohol* 44, no. 6 (1983): 950.

21. Elma VanLuven, "Effects of Parent-Child Dyads on Self-Image and Mate Selection," *Dissertation Abstracts International* 42 (1984): 1067.

22. Frank Minirth and Paul Meier, *Happiness Is a Choice* (Grand Rapids: Baker, 1978).

23. David Stoop, *Living with a Perfectionist* (Nashville: Thomas Nelson, 1987). An important book we feel will have a tremendous impact on people with low self-worth.

24. Lee Courtland, "Predicting Career Choice Attitudes," *Vocational Guidance Quarterly* 32, no. 3 (1984): 177.

25. Minirth and Meier, *Happiness Is a Choice*, 149.

26. N. J. Anastasiow, "Success in School and Boys' Sex-role Patterns," *Child Development* 36 (1978): 1053–66.

27. H. B. Biller, "Father Absence and the Personality Development of the Male Child," *Developmental Psychology* 11 (1978): 181–201.

28. Brian Lucas, "Identity Status, Parent-Adolescent Relationships, and Participation in Marginal Religious Groups," *Dissertation Abstracts International* 43, no. 12-B (1984): 4131.

29. J. V. Mitchell, "Goal-Setting Behavior as a Function of Self-Acceptance, Over- and Under-Achievement and Related Personality Variables," *Journal of Educational Psychology* 50 (1970): 93–104. As part of our research for this book, we did a computer search at Arizona State University, and for the years 1980 through 1986, the data base pulled up 12,432 studies directly related to the study of self-concept.

30. Matthew 22:37, 39.

31. Proverbs 24:33–34.

Chapter 2

1. William F. Arndt and R. Wilbur Gingrich, eds., *A Greek-English Lexicon of the New Testament and Other Early Christian Literature* (Chicago: University of Chicago Press, 1957), 119.

2. Ibid., 120.

3. Ibid.

4. Things like coming home late without calling, failing a course, talking back, and so on.

5. See also Proverbs 3:9; John 5:23.

6. Arndt and Gingrich, *Lexicon*, 825.

7. Gerhard Kittel and Gerhard Friedrich, eds., *Theological Dictionary of the New Testament* (Grand Rapids: Eerdmans, 1972), 170.

8. In the book of Ezekiel, the word *honor* is used to stand for "treasures" of silver and gold that were stolen from the people. See also Numbers 22:17, 37.

9. R. Laird Harris, *Theological Workbook of the Old Testament, Volume 1* (Chicago: Moody Press, 1980), 426.

10. For a very challenging look at how God's glory should motivate us to honor and praise, see John Piper's *Desiring God: Meditations of a Christian Hedonist* (Portland: Multnomah Press, 1986). Don't be thrown off by the subtitle. It's an excellent book for those who want to learn more about worshiping God.

11. The same thing is true in a marriage. Time after time in counseling, we see a couple where one or both parties have "no feelings whatsoever" for the other person. But if they'll treat each other like a priceless treasure, within a few weeks, very often their positive feelings for each other will come back! Just by getting couples to act on this one fact, we've seen the Lord restore relationships that looked beyond repair.

12. Kittel and Friedrich, *Theological Dictionary*, 171.

13. J. H. Moulton and George Milligan, *The Vocabulary of the Greek Testament: Illustrated from the Papyri and Other Non-Literary Sources* (Grand Rapids: Eerdmans, 1974), 635.

14. A. D. Noch, "Studies in the Graeco-Roman Beliefs of the Empire," *Harvard Studies in Classical Philology* 41 (1958): 252.

15. Hebrews 3 and 5.

16. H. G. Liddell and Robert Scott, *An Intermediate Greek-English Lexicon* (Oxford: Oxford University Press, 1975), 808.

17. Psalms 63:6; 77:11.

Chapter 3

1. Deuteronomy 5:16.

2. E. Hooker, "The Adjustment of the Male Overt Homosexual," *Journal of Projective Techniques* 27 (1967): 18–21; C. A. Trip, *The Homosexual Matrix* (New York: McGraw-Hill, 1975); and many other findings.

3. William S. Appleton, *Fathers and Daughters* (New York: Berkley Books, 1984), 171.

4. C. S. Lewis once wrote of God's masculine characteristics, "In comparison to God, everyone is feminine." "Notes on the Way," *Time and Tide* 29 (1948): 14.

5. Deuteronomy 5:16.

6. To our doctor or nurse friends, please don't scream as you read this. We've tried to explain this complicated process very simply and draw a practical application from it.

7. Neil R. Carlson, *Physiology of Behavior* (Boston: Allyn & Bacon, 1977), 11.

8. By the way, as short-distance joggers, we can verify that this is a wise decision for anyone being chased by a dog.

9. John M. Davis, "Models of Affective Disorders Due To Stress," *Neuropsychopharmacology* 6 (1984): 192.

10. Albert A. Kurtland, "Biochemical and Emotional Interaction in the Etiology of Cancer," *Psychiatric Research Review* 35 (1978): 25.

11. Psalm 119:105.

12. Adapted from Matthew 6:21.

13. Gary Smalley and John Trent, *The Blessing* (Nashville: Thomas Nelson, 1986), 219ff.

14. Our thanks to Tim Kimmel at Generation Ministries for explaining this concept to us as part of his excellent upcoming book, *Finding Rest in a Restless World*.

15. Marshall Goodman, "Divorce Takes Its Toll," *USA Today*, September 14, 1986.

16. Ibid.

Chapter 4

1. Hebrews 12:5ff.; James 1:2.

2. For a challenging look at the need to honestly confront problems rather than try to avoid them, see M. Scott Peck, *The Road Less Traveled* (New York: Simon & Schuster, 1978).

3. Romans 5:3; Hebrews 12:10ff.; James 1.

4. Arndt and Gingrich, *Lexicon*, 157.

5. Matthew 18:6.

6. Matthew 22:36–40; Romans 8:28; 1 Timothy 1:5.

7. Genesis 37–50.

8. Genesis 50:20, italics added.

9. Isaiah 61:3.

10. Psalm 119:105.

11. Since we saw him on television, David's inspiring story has come out in book form: David Rover, *Welcome Home, Davie* (Waco: Word Books, 1986).
12. Ibid.

Chapter 5
1. William Shakespeare, *Romeo and Juliet*, Act II, Scene 2, Line 1.
2. Gary Collins, *How to Be A People Helper* (Santa Ana, Calif.: Vision House, 1976), 33.
3. 1 Samuel 19:1ff.
4. 2 Samuel 1:12ff.
5. 2 Samuel 6:16.
6. 2 Samuel 15:1ff.
7. 2 Samuel 11:1ff.
8. See chapters 9 through 12 on establishing loving boundaries for children.
9. Evert F. Harrison, ed., *Baker's Dictionary of Theology* (Grand Rapids: Baker, 1960), 257.
10. C. S. Lewis, *The Problem of Pain* (New York: MacMillan, 1946), 69.

Chapter 6
1. Matthew 15:1ff.; Mark 7:5ff.; Luke 5:30–32.
2. Matthew 16:21–23; John 18:10; Matthew 26:69–75.
3. Proverb 10:19.
4. Isaiah 50:7.
5. Luke 7:34.
6. Proverbs 2:1–9; 9:8ff.

Chapter 8
1. M. Rands, "Implicit Theories of Relationships," *Journal of Personality and Social Psychology* 37 (1979): 645–61.
2. James J. Lynch, *The Language of the Heart* (New York: Basic Books, 1985).
3. Ibid., 225.
4. Proverbs 18:21.
5. Joe Bayly, *The Last Thing We Talk About* (Chicago: Cook, 1973).

6. Our missions statement for *Today's Family* is based on the greatest commandment; our goal is to motivate people to highly value God and others and to see their own value in Christ.

7. William Sears, "Your Responsive Baby," *Family Life Today*, 12, no. 4 (1986): 30.

8. Ibid., 30.

9. Carol Kuykendall, *Learning to Let Go* (Grand Rapids: Zondervan, 1985); Gary Smalley, *The Key to Your Child's Heart* (Waco, Tex.: Word, 1984).

10. Guy Mecklin, "Always Up to Bat," *Sports Illustrated*, October 1986.

11. Gordon McDonald, *Ordering Your Private World* (Nashville: Thomas Nelson, 1985).

Chapter 9

1. Genesis 3:1ff.

2. Genesis 12:20.

3. Genesis 18:13.

4. Numbers 20:11–12.

5. Francis Brown, S. R. Driver, and Charles A. Briggs, *A Hebrew and English Lexicon of the Old Testament* (Oxford: Clarendon Press, 1974), 407.

6. Arndt and Gingrich, *Lexicon*, 247.

7. R. W. White, "Self-Concept and School Adjustment," *Personnel and Guidance Journal* 46 (1976): 478–81.

8. Kittel and Friedrich, *Theological Dictionary*, 49.

Chapter 10

1. Elton Trueblood, *Abraham Lincoln: Theologian of American Anguish* (New York: Harper & Row, 1971), 171.

2. Proverb 19:5.

3. Erwin W. Lutzer, *The Necessity of Ethical Absolutes* (Grand Rapids: Zondervan, 1981).

4. William Lewis, *Coming Home* (New York: Harper and Row, 1986), 211.

Chapter 11

1. Our special thanks to Dr. Jeffrey M. Trent, associate professor at the University of Arizona Medical School, for his help in explaining this concept to us.

2. Our thanks to Rev. John Werhaus who first illustrated to us the importance of asking and answering these four questions.

3. Isaiah 14 and Ezekiel 28 both speak of Satan's fall because he claimed a position he didn't hold. Others have followed his lead down through the years.

4. David G. Myers, "The Inflated Self," *The Christian Century* 18 (1974): 1226–30.

5. Ibid.

6. John 3:16.

7. Deuteronomy 7:6.

8. Matthew 13:46.

9. Psalm 8:5.

10. Romans 8:37–39.

11. 1 Peter 2:9.

12. Genesis 1:27.

13. Matthew 6:26.

14. Ephesians 2:4–5.

15. See chapter 17 on offering honor to God.

16. Hans Walter Wolff, *Anthropology of the Old Testament* (Philadelphia: Fortress Press, 1974), 23.

17. See chapters 15 and 16 on the dark side of loyalties.

Chapter 12

1. 1 Samuel 14:24ff.

2. Arndt and Gingrich, *Lexicon*, 825.

3. For more information on setting up contracts with your children, see Gary's book, *The Key to Your Child's Heart*, "Balancing Loving Support Through Contracts," 77ff.

Chapter 13

1. D. J. Owens, "The Social Structure of Violence in Childhood," *Aggressive Behavior* 12 (1975): 68.

2. Clyde S. Kilby, ed., *An Anthology of C. S. Lewis: A Mind Awake* (New York: Harcourt, Brace & World, 1968), 73.

3. Brown, Driver, and Briggs, *Hebrew Lexicon*, 137.

4. Norman H. Smaith, *The Distinctive Ideas of the Old Testament* (London: Epworth Press, 1964), 118.

5. William L. Holladay, *A Concise Hebrew and Aramaic Lexicon of the Old Testament* (Grand Rapids: Eerdmans, 1971), 113.

6. See Appleton, *Fathers and Daughters*, 81.

7. Brown, Driver, and Briggs, *Hebrew Lexicon*, 137.
8. James Tramill, "The Relationship Between Type A and Type B Behavior Patterns and Level of Self-Worth," *Psychological Record* 35 (1985): 323–27.
9. D. C. Glass, "Behavior Patterns and Stress Management," *American Journal of Medicine* 108 (1981): 55–59.
10. NBC Evening News, September 11, 1986.
11. Romans 5:6ff.

Chapter 14

1. S. A. Coopersmith, "A Method for Determining Types of Self-Esteem," *Journal of Abnormal and Social Psychology* 59 (1967): 459.
2. Ibid.
3. On opening and closing a child's spirit, see Gary's *The Key to Your Child's Heart*, "How to Overcome the Major Destroyer of Families," 1ff.
4. See chapters 9 through 12 on establishing loving boundaries.
5. Genesis 3:9–13; 4:6–12.
6. Proverb 14:8.

Chapter 15

1. Exodus 20:5.
2. Romans 8:37.
3. Leviticus 16.
4. Alfred Edershime, *The Life and Times of Jesus the Messiah, Part One* (Grand Rapids: Eerdmans, 1972), 103.
5. For a chilling look at such a parent, see M. Scott Peck, *People of the Lie* (New York: Simon & Schuster, 1983).

Chapter 16

1. James Dobson, *Love Must Be Tough* (Waco: Word Books, 1983).
2. Acts 24:25.
3. Wilder Penfield, *The Mystery of the Mind* (Princeton: Princeton University Press, 1977), 148.
4. Dobson, *Love Must Be Tough*.
5. K. E. Moyer, "Kinds of Aggression and Their Physiological Basis," *Communications in Behavioral Biology* 2 (1968): 65–87.

6. Gary Smalley, *Joy That Lasts* (Grand Rapids: Zondervan, 1986).

7. See chapters 4 and 5 on finding value in troubled times.

Chapter 17

1. C. S. Lewis, *The Weight of Glory* (Grand Rapids: Eerdmans, 1949), 10.

2. Romans 2:23.

3. Charles Swindoll, *Growing Deep in the Seasons of Life* (Portland: Multnomah Press, 1985).

4. Acts 24:25–26.

5. Gordon MacDonald's book, *Restoring Your Spiritual Passion*, and Swindoll's book on *Growing Deep in the Seasons of Life*.